WITHDRAWN

WILLIAM MEYEROWITZ

WILLIAM MEYEROWITZ
The Artist Speaks

THERESA BERNSTEIN MEYEROWITZ

PHILADELPHIA: THE ART ALLIANCE PRESS
NEW YORK • LONDON • TORONTO: CORNWALL BOOKS

© 1986 by Associated University Presses, Inc.

Associated University Presses
440 Forsgate Drive
Cranbury, NJ 08512

Associated University Presses
25 Sicilian Avenue
London WC1A 2QH, England

Associated University Presses
2133 Royal Windsor Drive
Unit 1
Mississauga, Ontario
Canada L5J 1K5

Library of Congress Cataloging in Publication Data

Bernstein, Theresa.
　William Meyerowitz, the artist speaks.

　1. Meyerowitz, William, 1887–1981.　2. Artists—
United States—Biography.　I. Title.
N6537.M49M48　1986　　　760'.092'4　[B]　　84-45010
ISBN 0-87982-513-8 (Art Alliance)
ISBN 0-8453-4768-3 (Cornwall Books)

Printed in the United States of America

Contents

Foreword by James B. Bell		7
Preface		9
Acknowledgments		10
1	Childhood in Russia	13
2	Immigration to the United States and Student Days	17
3	Our Meeting and Marriage	23
4	Gloucester and Folly Cove	28
5	Our First Trip to Europe, 1922	34
6	Gloucester, 1923	39
7	The Whitney Studio Club—The Art Scene	46
8	Our Friends, Students, and Collectors	53
9	Justices of the Supreme Court	60
10	Mexico	65
11	Israel	69
12	The Art of William Meyerowitz	73
Appendix A: One-Man Exhibitions		85
Appendix B: Permanent Collections and Awards		87
Appendix C: Excerpts from Commentaries on the Works of William Meyerowitz		89
Appendix D: Comments by the Artist on His Work		94
Index		95
List of Reproductions		97
Illustrations: Works by William Meyerowitz		101

Foreword
William Meyerowitz (1887–1981)

IN THE FALL OF 1983, THE NEW-YORK HISTORICAL SOCIETY HAD THE HONOR OF PRESENTING the work of two prominent New York artists in the exhibition, "New York Themes: Paintings and Prints by William Meyerowitz and Theresa Bernstein." The two artists had for over one-half century lived on Manhattan's Upper West Side, site of the Society's building, where Mrs. Meyerowitz resides still. Displaying their work in a museum they had frequented and enjoyed many times over the years was gratifying for both Mrs. Meyerowitz and her neighbors here at The New-York Historical Society.

William and Theresa Bernstein Meyerowitz were very much in the center of New York's community of artists, and they crossed paths with an astonishing variety of now famous American artists.

Meyerowitz helped form the People's Art Guild with Robert Henri and George Bellows and counted among his friends artists of such different schools as Oscar Bluemner, Marsden Hartley, John Marin, Jan Matulka, Mark Rothko, and John Sloan. Louise Nevelson took art classes from Meyerowitz and Bernstein in New York. The couple exhibited their works together with those of their good friends William and Marguerite Zorach in a "couples" exhibition and attended Gertrude Vanderbilt Whitney's soirees, so popular among many of their fellow artists.

Meyerowitz, a "gentle modernist," was born in Russia in 1887 and immigrated to New York with his family in 1908. He studied at the National Academy of Design from 1912 to 1916 and devoted himself also to the art of etching. His work was first seen in a public exhibition in 1918, when examples were included in the Brooklyn Museum's third Annual Exhibition. In 1923, he had a one-man exhibition of his black-and-white and color etchings at the Smithsonian Institution's United States National Museum. Meyerowitz was the etcher featured in the Fox Film Company's 1925 film called "The Magic Needle," the first educational film about etching ever produced. Until his death in 1981, Meyerowitz's work was included regularly in group exhibitions, and he had frequent one-man shows.

Meyerowitz was immersed in classical music. While a student at the National Academy of Design, he helped support himself by singing in the chorus of the Metropolitan Opera. "My musical education was of considerable enlightenment in my understanding of the relationship between music and painting," he said. "The artist improvises with paint on canvas much the same as the pianist finds expression with the keyboard of his instrument." Perhaps because of his love for and understanding of music (which he shared with his friend Isaac Stern), Meyerowitz often received praise for the lyrical qualities of his works and their careful composition.

While his early etchings display an atmospheric mood similar to the works of James Abbott McNeill Whistler *(Grant's Tomb)*, he experimented with the fracturing of forms in a cubist manner in some of his New York cityscapes *(New York, No. 1)*. At the same time, expressionism, the transmitting of the artists' feelings into their works without concern for the representation of actual physical forms, was of interest to him, though his works never completely abandon recognizable forms. His love of music must have contributed to his interest in expressionism. From 1940 to 1945 he taught painting and etching at the Modern School of Self-Expression in the Bronx.

Both Meyerowitz and Bernstein (they were married in 1919) were accomplished portraitists. They frequently painted self-portraits and portraits of each other. Meyerowitz etched a series of portraits of Supreme Court Justices, including Justice Oliver Wendell Holmes. Bernstein can remember painting a portrait of her husband and Stuart Davis as they sat over a game of chess in their Gloucester studio. Both husband and wife produced portraits of Professor Albert Einstein.

Because of their subject matter, many of Meyerowitz's etchings and paintings now have an importance to those who seek to see how New York once looked. A glimpse of his life helps us to understand the richness of the art community in New York during the first three-quarters of this century. When seen as a whole through the eyes of his wife in this splendid memoir, Meyerowitz's works represent two of the most popular characteristics of American art: the style is clear and representational and only occasionally swerves to reflect contemporary stylistic trends; the subjects, in general, are sensitive and often poignant depictions of American life.

James B. Bell, Director
The New-York Historical Society

Preface

WILLIAM MEYEROWITZ WAS BORN IN THE LITTLE TOWN OF GEZELITZ NEAR EKATERINO-slav, in the Ukraine, possibly in 1887. At an early age he felt that his destiny was to be an artist. Circumstances propelled him to the strange new land of America, where by the power of his talent, vision, and dedication, he achieved the stature of a major artist.

His personality was like a magnet that drew interesting people to him. His firm handclasp, engaging smile, and natural reticence made him a delightful companion to all who met him. His talent was appreciated by prominent men including Supreme Court Justice Oliver Wendell Holmes, who gave Meyerowitz his first portrait commission. This was followed by commissions from the other members of the Supreme Court of the 1920s. Prior to that, Meyerowitz had won Honorable Mention of the Prix de Rome in 1917 for his mural painting *Drama as a Teacher,* at the School of the National Academy of Design. His musical talent enabled him to sing in the chorus of the Metropolitan Opera House, and he spoke seven languages. While working as an architect, he helped design the first concrete high-rise building in New York.

Meyerowitz was one of the founders of the People's Art Guild, an association whose members also included George Bellows and Robert Henri and whose goal was to bring art to the people. He pioneered the first etchings in color by a unique new process. The Fox Film Company asked him to demonstrate this process of etching in a documentary film called *The Magic Needle* in 1925. Requested to do a portrait of Albert Einstein, Meyerowitz interpreted the great scientist in a memorable study. He was invited as an artist to record the first Zionist meeting in the United States, which took place at Madison Square Garden in 1923. Meyerowitz was elected a director of Independent Artists, an organization that flourished in the United States after World War I. In 1930 he was commissioned by the Jefferson Foundation to paint and etch the home of James Monroe, "Ashlawn," and the home of Thomas Jefferson, "Monticello," as well as the University of Virginia. The Smithsonian Institution invited him to exhibit his work in 1923 and again in 1941. In 1942 he won the First Prize from the American Color Print Society for his original process of etching in color. The National Academy of Design elected him to be a member in 1943. In 1940 *Current Biography* published the story of his career, along with biographies of Thomas Mann and Jan Pierce. Modern Artists of Boston awarded Meyerowitz the Mittengold Medal for his painting, *Exodus,* in 1944, and the Joseph Pennell Prize was given to him by the Library of Congress in 1944. He won the Ellen Speyer Prize at the National Academy of Design in 1944 for *Horseback Riders.* He was a member of the Arts Council of the City of Gloucester, and a director of the

North Shore Arts Association (Gloucester), and he was elected an Honorary Member in 1950. In 1952 he was elected the president of the Friends of Zion II, the first Zionist organization in America, and a member of the Manhattan Chapter of B'nai Zion, an outgrowth of that organization. He received the Honorary Membership and Gold Medal of the Academy of Parma, Italy, in 1980, and he was posthumously awarded the Academy of Europe Award in 1983.

With the profound impact of his personality hovering over my consciousness, I was determined to bring the echo of my deep perception of my late husband into concrete form. I suddenly had a revelation that spoke to me. It said, "You must write this book."

—Theresa Bernstein, 1984

Acknowledgments

I WISH TO ACKNOWLEDGE MY APPRECIATION TO THE FOLLOWING PEOPLE WHO HAVE helped me to complete this book:

Linda Ellis, Timothy Gray, Helen McKammy, Pamlyn Smith, Richard Talbert, Judith Van Damm, and Patricia Waller.

To Inez Metzl for her typing;

To all the other people who have shown interest;

To Dana Thomas and David Wise for their editorial assistance.

WILLIAM MEYEROWITZ

Father, Gershon Ben Zion Meyerowitz, and Grandfather, Philadelphia 1895

1
Childhood in Russia

A TALL MAN IN A LONG BLACK COAT WAS WALKING HOME ACROSS A LITTLE BRIDGE IN Gezelitz, a village in the Ukraine. Approaching him and blowing in the wind was a large sign with two small legs visible below. As he got closer, the man recognized his own son.

"What are you doing here?"

The young boy looked up. "We've just finished the sign and I'm bringing it to the baker."

The astonished father said, "Be sure to come home early. It's the Sabbath."

Without his father's knowledge, William had been working for a sign painter for some time. He mixed the paints and became fascinated when he was given the job to decorate a tin bed with wreaths of flowers and singing birds. In return, the sign painter gave William little pieces of canvas and some colors for his own use.

As Gershon, William's father, continued his journey, he met the rabbi, who said, "How is it that your son only comes to school a couple of days a week? Why doesn't he attend classes like the other children?"

Again the father was amazed, and when he saw William he demanded, "What have you been doing? I told the rabbi that you went out every morning after breakfast and came home in time for dinner."

William was forced to admit that he had been in the attic and that he had a whole cache of drawings which he had made in secret there.

The father gave him the "dose" he deserved and then said, "My son, bring me all your sketches and I will show them to the Rabbi tomorrow, after the Sabbath, and find out what he thinks."

The next day William listened at the keyhole as his father conferred with the rabbi behind a locked door. William heard the Rabbi say, "To be an artist is very, very hard. By the time he paints a little bird, he will eat up a horse."

Horses were also one of William's fascinations. Every morning the farmers would come with their horse-drawn wagons and vegetables to sell in the market. William would go to the market and watch the horses. One day he went over to a horse to pat it on the nose. The horse got scared and bit him on the hand, and there was a great uproar. William was taken home where his hand was bandaged and he was put to bed. But not for long because within a couple of days he was back in the marketplace, sketching the horses.

The boy pursued his drawing with exuberance. He explored every facet of village life with his pencil and pad. He loved to watch the people coming into his grandfather's garden, which was on the edge of the Dnieper River. There were little bathhouses on the river's edge and, for a few coins, people could bathe in the river. For sport, William took the horses that belonged to the neighbors and drove them into the water, holding onto their manes as they paddled along.

The exact day or year of William's birth was not recorded, but his mother remembered that he was born on a Thursday night when she was preparing noodles for the next day's Sabbath meal. And, she said, it was the middle of summer. So it was decided that July 15 was to be his birthday—which later proved to be the date of Rembrandt's birth as well. William's birthdate is not known, but it may have been 1887. William was the oldest of the six children born to Shendl and Gershon Meyerowitz. Gershon was a cantor. There were two more boys, Nathan, and the youngest child, James, and three girls, Sophie, Bessie, and Minna.

Music came naturally to the young boy. He heard his father singing at home and in the synagogue. Under his father's tutelage, William's knowledge of music was augmented. His singing was so fine that people said he would be eligible for a scholarship to the Music Conservatory.

Village life was usually calm and pleasant, but for the Jews there was always the lingering fear of a pogrom, and one night one occurred. Early in the evening, William was coming home from the sign painter's shop when he heard the smashing of windows and the splitting of doors. Panic stricken, he hid behind a barrel in the backyard, and as the peasants rushed by with their lanterns, William scurried away on his hands and knees. His mother had climbed into a carriage with her youngest child. She told the driver to take her all around the village because it would be hours before they could return home in safety.

When it was over the family wondered, "What shall we do? Is this going to be another exodus?"

But quiet returned to the village, and the routine of life resumed. William, then ten years old, continued to work for the sign painter. Next door to the sign painter, was a photographer's shop. William was fascinated by this process. He watched the photographer taking pictures. He was able to convince the photographer to lend him an old camera, which William brought home. He sat his mother in a big armchair for her photograph, with a footstool for her feet. She wore a very fine Sabbath dress. Then he decided to take a photograph of himself. He put the menorah on the table and donned his little *talis*—prayer shawl—and the skull cap or *yarmulke* that he always wore when he went to the synagogue to sing with the children. He managed to put the camera on another table, and with a long pipe and a bulb, he took this picture.

William's grandfather had a little shop in which he sold oil for stoves and heating, herring, and other commodities that the peasants came to buy. His grandfather was a devout person who went to the synagogue often. William would be taken along, and he would snuggle in the folds of his grandfather's *talis*, listening to the lilt and droning of the Hebrew chanting as the congregation prayed at sunrise. In those days the Jewish children were not permitted to study in the Russian schools. The only exception to this rule was for a rich family in which the father would be able to pay for eight other non-Jewish students. William received his early education in the *cheder*, the Hebrew school that was taught by the rabbi. The books were the Talmud. The students became well versed in the Old Testament. This background was to serve William throughout his artistic career in his depictions of Hebraic themes.

William's grandmother did most of the housework. Early in the morning she would prepare to go to the market. She would get out of bed at dawn, say the prayers, and share breakfast with the children. She would eat the soft part of their bread, and give the crust to William, and then they would go out.

William's grandfather was called *Lebovitch Schvartze* which means, "Levy the Dark One." He was a very pious man. One day he was sitting in front of his shop and a stranger came over to him. "I've inquired everywhere for an honest man, and everybody here tells me that you are the most honest, the most reliable person, whom anyone could trust. My name is Nobel."

His grandfather had been reading the Torah. Interrupted, he looked up in annoyance and said, "Pferd, wer fregt bei dir?"—"Horse, who's asking you?"

After a bit of misunderstanding, the stranger was finally accepted. It turned out that he was a representative of the firm of Nobel, purveyors of oils. In fact, this Nobel is the source of the Nobel Prizes. Mr. Nobel was looking for a merchant to handle his products and this conversation resulted in the grandfather's getting the franchise.

As an education was so difficult to obtain in the village, the nearby town of Kiev was the seat of learning to which scholars would go for advanced investigations and discussions of the Talmud. The Talmud was the basis of debate on Jewish law and posed questions such as: if the wheels of a wagon were to turn on the Sabbath, would it be right or would it be wrong?

At the appropriate age William was bar mitzvah, which means he was accepted by his peers in the synagogue and given the opportunity to be an individual, responsible for his own acts and moral behavior. His grandfather had wished him to be a rabbi, and when he saw that William's inclination was to be an artist, he felt that he had been catering to a lost soul, that William would surely depart from the fold.

It was decided that William's brother Nathan should attend the local agricultural school, and a large fee was requested. William offered some of his drawings in place of this fee. When the school officials saw these drawings, they accepted a group of them as payment for Nathan's schooling for a semester.

In those early days William could not afford to buy shoes. He would cut them out of cardboard and wrap rags around his feet so he could walk on the streets of his village.

After school his friends would jump on William because he was very sturdy and strong, even though he was quite short. They would tousle him and fight with him, sometimes three or four at once. One day William gave one of the boys a powerful punch, and when he saw the blood coming from the child's nose, he resolved never to fight again.

The Russian authorities were harsh in their behavior toward the Jewish community and weeded out anybody they suspected of antigovernment activities. One afternoon William was standing in front of a coffeehouse where a group of older boys were meeting. William had no idea what the gathering was about but, curious, he had followed the boys who were now standing outside. One of the youths pushed leaflets into his hand. As William had no education in Russian, he could not read it and had no notion of what the leaflets said. A policeman suddenly appeared and shouted, "Come with me!" He took William to jail and booked him along with the other young men who had been seized inside the coffeehouse. William was incarcerated for a couple of weeks before his family was able to obtain his release. He described the jail as a place where there were no beds. Everyone slept on two sloping boards—one on one side and one on the other side—like the roof of a house. The windows were only little slits in the wall, but he could stand up and look out and see what was going on in the courtyard. Once a day they were fed soup and some soggy bread. It was like the description of a prison that Pasternak later wrote in *Dr. Zhivago*. His father was finally able to get him out by explaining to the police that the leaflets had been forced into the boy's hand and that William had nothing to do with the group or its activities.

After one more pogrom—in which William's best friend was killed by a bullet from the revolver of a Russian peasant, the family decided it was time for William to leave Russia. His father and grandfather had already gone to the United States. Now Gershon came to get William.

Securing a passport was not an easy matter for the family. If there had been public records, the boys would have been forced into the army. One had to maneuver with cunning. The government did not issue passports to Jews and there were no birth certificates. Many young Jewish boys had been kidnapped by the army and kept away from their families for twenty years. They lost all track of their backgrounds and often they would be just faintly aware of their origins. William used to sing a song about this.

A passport was procured for William from an older man, a form of protection for William to prevent his being taken away. Then the family managed to sneak across the border. From Liebau, in Lithuania, they took a boat for the "Promised Land."

2

Immigration to the United States and Student Days

WILLIAM AND HIS FATHER CAME TO THE UNITED STATES AS IMMIGRANTS, LEAVING THE rest of the family behind. They took a room on the lower East Side of New York, possibly on Orchard Street, where they could hear the familiar Yiddish spoken and try to find their balance in the New World. Seeing the pushcarts and markets and his people in his new land, William felt almost at home. He continued to make drawings of all he saw.

The first time William went into the subway he watched the crowds. At the Brooklyn Bridge, people were running in huge masses, all in one direction. Thinking that something had happened, William ran along. Suddenly those people disappeared, and another wave of humanity emerged and ran in the other direction. He joined the second group, but then he realized they were commuters going to or from their trains.

In search of a job, William went to see Mr. Trud, who had been the president of the synagogue where he had been an alto as a boy of ten. Mr. Trud was an engineer and a builder. He listened to William's voice and said, "No, I cannot get you a job as a singer. Your voice is changing."

As Mr. Trud was constructing the first buildings in cement, much against the wishes of the bricklayers, he decided that perhaps he could give William a job as a night watchman. He found William a room with his own parents that was close to the building site.

After a couple of nights, Mr. Trud was feeling nervous about William, and he decided to walk over at midnight to see how his young charge was doing. As he neared the hut on Riverside Drive at 138th Street, he sensed that a meal was being prepared. He opened the door, and there was William with a pot on a stove, cooking bones for borscht. Mr. Trud joined William and they shared a midnight repast. Mr. Trud learned that William was talented in art and got him a few jobs decorating the vestibules of apartment buildings that he controlled. In one was a scene with birch trees, and in another people on a boat floating on the Dnieper River.

Self-Portrait, Age Eleven

Mr. McKenna, an architect friend of Mr. Trud's, needed an assistant, and William was given the job. There he gained experience erecting building models from blueprints. As William was good at proportions and perspective, it wasn't long before Mr. McKenna turned over most of the important projects to his young assistant.

Riding on the train one day, William observed a boy with a paintbox. The idea struck William that the boy was an art student, and William asked him where he was going. But the student refused to answer and simply turned his head away. William watched

Self-Portrait as Cantor

the student get off the subway and followed him, walking behind until the boy reached the National Academy of Design School, on 109th Street and Amsterdam Avenue. That was exactly what William wanted to find. He registered and became a student at the school.

William had a fine baritone voice. When he saw an advertisement for chorus singers at the Metropolitan Opera, he applied and was accepted. He was skilled in reading

 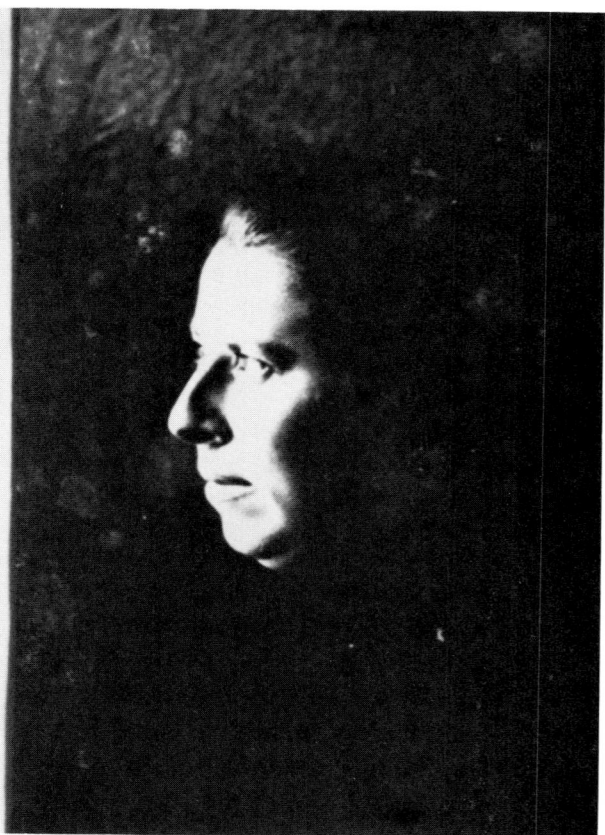

William's Father, taken by William **William's Mother, Shendl , taken by William**

music, and he had learned to read German, Italian, French, and Russian. Even though it had not been possible to study Russian when he lived in the Ukraine, William had picked it up from Mr. Trud's Russian friends. The Metropolitan Opera's chorus coach, Mr. Morgenstern, said to William, "These horses can hardly pronounce German, but you're good at it." William became a leader for the rest of the chorus. This was during the era of the great Enrico Caruso, who sang "La Juive" and other famous roles. Geraldine Farrar, another renowned singer of the period, starred in *The Girl of the Golden West*. William was in the chorus of these operas, and in Wagner's youthful masterpiece, *Die Meistersinger*, William appeared as one of the apprentices. Working night and day for several years, William finally was able to earn enough money to pay for his family's transportation to the United States. On the East Side he found a railroad flat that was big enough to accommodate the entire family. William lived at home and paid the rent. Since there were five other children, William contributed as much as he could.

William was given a printing press, which he set up in one of the rooms, and this became the print room. When his brother Nathan would come in to discuss his love affairs or would-be love affairs, he would sit down on the prints and talk away. William would chase him out of the room saying, "I'll talk to you later. Look what you've done!"

The apartment included a parlor—this was before the advent of the living room. The walls all contained William's unframed paintings, which included portraits of the family—one of his uncle Moshe, his mother's brother, whom William idolized. The subject of another painting was a court scene in which a family was waiting for the father to be made a citizen of the United States. This painting contained a portrait of Lincoln on one side and of George Washington on the other. All these early paintings disappeared because they were given to tradesmen by the family in lieu of payment of debts the family had incurred at the greengrocer or at the butcher. Gershon died at fifty-two, and we were appointed guardians of his mother and five sisters and brothers.

William brought home a beautiful Oriental vase that was given him in exchange for some of his work. Wanting to share the treasure with his family, he placed the vase in front of the mantelpiece in the parlor where the girls received their boyfriends. They would dance to the music from a little phonograph, and one day they knocked over the vase and it broke into pieces. William said, "It's a telling blow, and I'm leaving home." He moved to Ridgefield, New Jersey, but he continued to pay the family's rent. And even though he had left them, they continued to idolize him as a brother and as the

Bill in Chorus of Metropolitan Opera, 1918

solver of all their problems. They would say, "William, oh, he can do anything."

William's middle sister, Bessie, married Ruel Stein, a building superintendent, and they had a son, Robert. Ruel suffered a fatal accident while on the job, and Bessie was griefstricken. William did everything imaginable, and after much trouble, he was able to convince the authorities to pay workman's compensation to the widow.

William painted his family. All of his three sisters were good-looking. Sophie was a brunette like William, Bessie was blonde with a rosebud complexion, and Minna too was blonde and was also musical. William made an etching of his two younger sisters sitting arm-in-arm. He was particularly interested in the motif of people joining arms and made drawings and paintings of couples walking arm-in-arm. He painted Sophie and etched her in many plates. He did a beautiful etching of his mother writing. His mother wrote letters to her son Nathan when he was in the army. William frequently chose his mother as his subject, and she was happy to pose for him ever since the first time he had photographed her. When he would win an award, she appreciated it with a smile.

The people and scenes he encountered were always the subjects of his drawings, paintings, and etchings. He made sketches of old men and women sitting on park benches, telling the stories of their lives to one another. He became intrigued with one shabbily dressed man standing on the corner selling shoelaces and asked if the man would like to pose for him. The man agreed.

At this time William was teaching drawing to students at the Federation Settlement House even though he was not paid for his efforts. At the Sunday class the students anticipated the appearance of the shoelace vendor, but when the man arrived he was clean-shaven, wearing a brand new suit and overcoat. At first William did not recognize him. "What has happened to your appearance?" he asked.

"You think I was going to let you draw me unshaven, in my old coat and hat, the one I wear every day in rain or shine?" exclaimed the vendor. "My son told me he was sure you were going to put me into motion pictures and that I'd better fix myself up."

William paid the man and sent him away because he was not at all interesting as a subject for painting without his beard, his little cap, and his tray of shoelaces.

William continued his training at the National Academy of Design. He won the Eliot Medal for Painting and Drawing and was selected to compete for the "Prix de Rome." He painted the mural *Drama as a Teacher* for this competiton, and he won First Honorable Mention for the mural, in 1916. In 1932 the mural was purchased by a lady who later refused to pay for it because her father objected to the nude in the center of the painting. William unsuccessfully sued, and the painting was returned; eventually it was sold to someone else. The First Prize in the Prix de Rome was three years of study in Rome. Russell Cowles won the prize and had been coached by William, so William decided he had studied at the Academy long enough and was ready to go out and look at nature on his own.

William took a shack in an art colony in Ridgefield, New Jersey. To get there it was necessary to board the ferry, cross the Hudson River, and then walk about a mile and a half to the bark-covered house. The house had no running water or heat, and he used an old stove. Whenever sections of the pipe collapsed, drenching the cabin in smoke, William would mount a chair and connect one section with another until the pipe reached the roof and the smoke went out properly through the chimney. There was a small porch with a magnificent view of the valley reaching to the foot of the Jersey hills.

3

Our Meeting and Marriage

P HILADELPHIA WAS MY HOMETOWN, WHERE MY FATHER WAS INVOLVED IN EXPERIMENTS IN the manufacture of artificial silk products. My mother was an accomplished musician, and at an early age I was drawing and painting. After I attended the Philadelphia School of Design and the Pennsylvania Academy of Art, my family moved to New York, where I studied at the Art Students League for a short time. I found a studio in the building known as the Holbein Studios, on West 55th Street. Below the studios were stables and it was necessary to climb up three steep flights of steps. There were four studios on the floor, each of which had a skylight, but no windows in the conventional sense, only a panel of glass that one pulled inwards to allow air to come into the room. Opposite my studio was one occupied by Michael Strange, the writer, who later married John Barrymore and became famous in her own right as a literary personage. For a party she was planning, she borrowed some draperies from my place to decorate the piano. At the party John Barrymore recited bits of Hamlet, his brother, Lionel Barrymore, read from a play, and Michael Strange read some of her poetry. Celebrities from the theatrical world crowded into her studio, and afterwards the frieze of empty wine bottles testified to the festivities.

At this time William was a member of the People's Art Guild, an organization led by Professor John Weischel, who was dedicated to bringing art to the people. William went around acquiring paintings to hang in a nearby settlement house so that poor children would be exposed to excellent art in their own environment. William had seen my work because I had been exhibiting for a couple of years, even though we had never met. He had the idea that I was an older woman and when I opened the door, he was surprised.

He inquired, "Is Theresa Bernstein in?"

"I'm Theresa Bernstein," I replied.

"I thought you were an old lady," was his reply.

In spite of this remark, I was instantly attracted to William. I felt as if the sun had burst into my little room. He was so earnest, so intense; his black hair shone like a halo around his head. He chose a couple of my paintings for the settlement house.

Neither William nor I had obtained a college degree. He had attended City College for a short time but did not continue, and I had won some scholarships for art and was completely absorbed in pursuing this. My higher education was largely derived from my reading in the libraries. Like Andrew Carnegie, I considered books the best means to study and grow, and I was frequently in the libraries, reading and doing research. In contrast to me, my mother had been very well educated. She knew all the classics, and she spoke three or four languages. She played the piano well and she was able to embroider. But whatever choices I made, my parents were completely satisfied. They assumed that I had enough sense to do the right thing.

For entertainment, William and I loved to go to the movies. Our favorite silent film personality was Charlie Chaplin. In the movie theater a piano would play and the captions would be provided under the pictures. While the romantic scenes went on, William would put my hand on his chest and hold it tightly. Although Chaplin's films were hilarious, they had a message underneath, and we were aware of it. He was making fun of the tyranny of machinery over man. We felt that too, and there were instances in our artwork when we expressed the same idea. One of our favorite films was the Marx Brothers' film of the 1930s, *A Night at the Opera*, which, with its high jinks and outrageous situations, was so funny.

After I became engaged to William, I went with my friend, Jean Oliver, to take a course in jewelry making. Jean wanted to make something for herself, but my objective was to make an engagement ring to give to William. Jean and I worked in the studio that had belonged to John Twachtman, who was one of the early artists in Gloucester. He always painted Gloucester in a misty veil of impenetrable morning dew.

The instructor, Grace Hazen, showed us how to make a ring. "You have to take a bar of silver and beat it with a round hammer until the ends come up to meet each other. Then you have to file off the edges to get them to meet. Finally, when you almost have it in a circle, you make a hole in the center of the bar. That will be for the insert of the stone," she explained.

I made a silver ring with a lapis lazuli stone set in. I draped silver wire around the stone to represent the rushing of waters, and the blue stone at the center represented a pool of still water.

We became engaged during World War I. William's brother Nathan was drafted into the army, and the very week when Bill's registration number was published in the newspaper, the armistice was declared. We celebrated by going to see the Armistice Day parade on 5th Avenue. We watched the parade from the window of an office of a friend on 5th Avenue and 42nd Street, opposite the library. He watched the flags of the nations fluttering in the breeze and a rain of paper from all the windows. People were happy. They hugged each other and said, "Peace, Peace, It's wonderful." William etched the parade, and I made drawings.

Soon the Jewish New Year came, and we went to the synagogue to hear William sing. He was the cantor in the synagogue near his family's apartment on 120th Street. Sitting with his three sisters, I saw William emerge on the pulpit in a white prayer shawl, with the high turban of white satin on his head. He was the baritone, while the tenor, the soprano, and the alto were in a little alcove above him. William had arranged most of the prayers they sang. His sisters turned to me and said, "Oh, he sings just like in the opera."

In 1919 we were married in New York City and we traveled by boat to Florida for our honeymoon. For a send-off, some friends gave us a big basket of fruit. We ate most of it, but we did not eat the oranges and grapefruits. A storm arose at sea, and it was a very

Bill and Theresa, 1919

rough trip. Objects were hurled from one side of the hold to the other, arousing even greater fear in the passengers. We heard two Chinese merchants in the next cabin praying, and we smelled their burning incense. I became violently seasick and kept thinking of Jonah and how he was tossed to the whale. To comfort me in my agony, William read passages from Milton's *Paradise Lost*. The following day the storm subsided, and I felt somewhat better. He then read to me from *Paradise Regained*.

We arrived in Jacksonville, Florida, carrying the basket of oranges and grapefruits, much to the hilarity of the passengers. It was truly a case of carrying coals to Newcastle.

We took a train and went to Avon Park, near Orlando. On the way, the train stopped at a station for a long time and I said, "It's sandy here, I should have gotten some sneakers."

Without a word, William dashed out and rushed up the hill to the street where the shops were. He came back with a pair of sneakers, but they were too large. I told him the right size and he rushed back again and went into the shop. The train conductor shouted, "All Aboard!" and the people on the train yelled, "Wait, wait! We're waiting for the sneakers!"

William returned and I tried on the sneakers and they were the right size. On the other side of the aisle, a couple was arguing. The woman said, "Would you do that for me?"

"Well, I don't know."

She said, "You *should* know."

When we arrived at Avon Park it was already evening. A music box was playing on the street. We left the hotel and waltzed on the pavement in the moonlight. Once in a while William would grab a little grapefruit from a tree over his head.

In the lobby a lady said, "I hope you'll help yourselves to grapefruits, there are so many. We have to shovel them into the ground every night because there are so many ripe fruits we don't know what to do with them."

The morning was fragrant with the smell of orange blossoms. We made drawings, and William made an etching of me. Again the hotel proprietor persuaded us to take all the grapefruits we could carry. I made a bag out of a knitted bathing suit of Bill's, by tying it in knots. In the grove we picked as many of the ripe fruits as we could fit into the bathing suit. William carried the package on his shoulders to bring upstairs. We didn't want to go through the lobby with this huge load so we climbed up the fire escape which passed the window where some guests were playing bridge. As we were climbing, the grapefruits started falling. I held the bag from below, but to no avail. They kept dropping out. When we got to our room, there were only three grapefruits left.

Just before I was to be married, I had found a two-room studio on West 67th Street that was more livable than the place I had lived in before. After we returned from Florida we lived there.

On weekends William took me out to his shack in Ridgefield, with the crackling wood stove and the frequently collapsing stovepipes that had to be adjusted so that we would not choke from the smoke. On the porch in the back, the thousand-leggers were rampant, and the well had a lot of garden snakes. To get water from the well it was necessary to remove the wooden lid and lower the bucket down to the water level, and pull it up. But after the effort, the water was fresh and clear.

The view from the rear of the cabin stretched for miles with the slope going down over the hills of New Jersey until they came to the flats. There were many young sapling trees and little sheds with goats. William made etchings of this scene. Sometimes we would get a big chunk of ice at the ferry station and carry it back. Unfortunately, the ice melted and not much was left by the time we got it home.

One day we had three visitors. They were girls, each weighing about 175 pounds, who were on a hike which they claimed was intended to help them lose weight. Appropriately dressed in khaki and sneakers, and carrying all the equipment, they arrived at our house so famished and exhausted that they devoured all the food they had with them, and whatever else they could find. I don't think they lost very much weight.

Dr. and Mrs. I. Hershfeld, close friends of William's, visited us at our cottage. (He was an orthodontist, who wrote a book called *The History of the Toothbrush*.) He photographed the interior and exterior of our little house as a memento. The pictures looked like a setting for a story by O. Henry.

In the spring we moved our effects to Gloucester, Massachusetts, where I had spent several summers.

4

Gloucester and Folly Cove

The Hawthorne Inn was in its heyday, and all society, or those who thought they were society, went there with their families for the summer. In the evening there was always entertainment—jugglers, dancers, and singers. In the lobby the ladies sat. We called them "The ladies of the Lobby." They had a view of who was coming in and who was going out and who was going with whom; what romance was flourishing and what marriage was breaking up. Like a jury in a box, with their lap dogs and their knitting, the women sat knitting and needling. Outside, there was a long porch where everybody would sit and watch the tennis players. At the end of the porch was a marvelous view of the ocean, the far horizon of Eastern Point with Cecelia Beaux's studio and Colonel Andrews's estate.

Among the artists who came to Hawthorne Inn at that time was Lewis Kronberg, a protégé of Mrs. Jack Gardner. He painted ballerinas. Eban Comins was also there, still painting society as society wished to be painted. These two men were popular bachelors. Whenever the inn needed an extra hand for bridge, they were there to fill the gap.

George Stacy, the proprietor of Hawthorne Inn, sat at his window at the entrance of the porch, watching everyone coming and going, like a captain at the bow of his ship. He let us use a little studio in one of the cottages where we could teach some of the summer residents who were eager to study with us. Our students included Jean Oliver, a critic for the *Boston Transcript*; Mrs. Banks, one of her friends; Emma Oliver; Mrs. Murphy from Baltimore; and Maidie Hooper, a member of the DAR, whose ancestors included one of the fifty-six signers of the Declaration of Independence. There was also Mrs. Wigglesworth and Margaret Hoyt, whose husband was the first cousin of President Wilson. Mrs. Hoyt suggested that after finishing the etching plates we should all go to Folly Cove where there was a printing press. The group grew quickly.

We would paint out in the open, near the road of the Hawthorne Casino, which was really a walk with shapely little trees that formed a natural protection against the sun.

Strollers-by would be seen, with their parasols flashing in and out of the network of trees. William made an etching of this scene. He called it *Sunday Morning,* and it was one of his very early etchings in color.

The casino at the end of the walk was a bustle of activity—it was a lecture hall in the early evenings, a dancehall at night, a church on Sunday morning. A section of the casino overlooked the street that was the Gallery for the Gloucester Society of Artists.

We met the president of the Society, Louise Brumback, at a tea given by Emmaline and William Atwood. Mr. Atwood had constructed the Gallery on the Moors, which had been designed by Herbert Adams Cram. It overlooked the whole harbor of Gloucester, including Hesperus Point, a view from which William made the etching *Out to Sea,* depicting the site of *The Wreck of the Hesperus* from Longfellow's poem.

Mr. and Mrs. Atwood were gracious hosts to many artists. The Gallery on the Moors was located on the very top of Ledge Road. All society came there to be seen and to look at the paintings, drawings, and etchings. Childe Hassam was among those invited, and John Singer Sargent came with Mrs. Gardner. Other artists who showed there were William Glackens and John Sloan. As there was a stage, actors and critics were also present. Visitors included Lillian Hellman, after finishing her play *The Little Foxes,* and Louis Hine, the art critic. William's *Gloucester Set* of paintings and etchings were shown there. My painting of *Bass Rocks Beach* was bought there by Lee Higginson. The gallery functioned until 1922, when it was overshadowed by the new society called The North Shore Arts Association, of which William and I were charter members.

The Atwoods gave an opening tea in the gallery. Fruit juice, called punch, was served in a large glass bowl. Usually, the punch contained stick, or hard liquor, and after a few glasses, people tended to become garrulous, omitting the barriers of class. The ladies were dressed especially for the occasion with large flowered hats, and Irish crocheted half-gloves, which were very much the style. Some of the gowns were dazzling with their flounces, high-boned collars in piqué or satin, and highbutton shoes. Sneakers, along with khaki, were considered the rage for the younger set. It was the last gasp of the corset era when women laced up, with heaving bustlines graduating to wine-glass waists. It was the fashion to have the Lillian Russell look. Many of the women carried parasols.

When the time came to print the etchings, we went to the Hales' in Folly Cove. Ellen Day Hale had a press, which she graciously offered to us.

The house where Ellen Day Hale lived was called "The Thickets." It was the ancestral home of the Reverend Edward Everett Hale, who wrote *The Man Without a Country.* Reverend Hale was a close friend of Emerson's, who visited "The Thickets." Edward Everett Hale had six sons, and Ellen Day Hale was his only daughter. One of the sons, Philip Hale, was a professor of painting at the Massachusetts Museum School, and his wife, Lillian Wescott Hale, was also an artist of note, a very fine painter. Philip Hale, who studied etching with William, said to William, "You ought to dress like an artist, with a long cape and pointed black shoes and pince-nez." William said, "You're referring to James McNeill Whistler." And they both laughed.

"The Thickets" was occupied by Ellen Day Hale and Gabrielle Devee Clemens, both artists. Ms. Clemens was the niece of Samuel Clemens, Mark Twain of American literature. Ms. Hale and Ms. Clemens had both studied in Paris and did many etchings in Italy.

At their studio William demonstrated the process of printing. We made this trip several times, until Ms. Hale offered us a little cottage at the edge of the shore. She said, "Why do you want to stay in East Gloucester and come here to print? It's such a long trip. We have a cottage you can occupy. You won't have to run out for all your meals.

Everything can be brought to you, and you can always have dinner with us." We accepted her offer, and moved to Folly Cove.

Our cottage was called "Gaviotta," which means "seagull" in Portuguese. As it was very dark inside, they suggested that we draw squares with white chalk wherever we wanted windows cut out of the walls. There was no electricity, but we had an oil lamp, and a kerosene stove for cooking.

There is a legend that the first shot of the American Revolution was fired at Folly Cove from an English frigate and that this might be the reason it was named "Folly Cove." However, one fact concerning the place is certain. It was the first location, and the important place, where William created his process of printing in color on the Hale press.

Just as we were moving into the cottage, William saw three women coming down the hill, carrying plates of fruit. A small child, with flowers in her hand, ran alongside the women. There was a knock on the door, as these women had come to greet their new neighbors. This motif became the etching in color called *The Three Generations.*

We could look out from Gaviotta and see the little Finnish girls dancing in a circle on the hill. William made studies of them.

We saw the beach with its great boulders where children played around in the water, swimming and hugging the stony eternity of the rocks. It was the place where Captain Burnham kept his lobster boat. He would sit for hours in the late afternoon sun holding the rope that held his boat to the shore. This was the beach where the rum runners had often come in the past to meet boats in the night. Where did they go? To the little Gaviotta, the cottage Ms. Hale had given to us. Often the searchlights of government vessels would flash on us at midnight to uncover secret meetings, which of course no longer took place while we were living there.

Nancy Hale, the small daughter of Philip and Lillian Hale, visited us one day. I told her, "I'm sorry the place is so upset!" She said, "Oh, I love messy rooms." Nancy had inherited the family talent for writing. Years later she wrote the plays *The Women* and *Life in the Studio,* which were based on the same Hale studio where we printed.

The Hales' home was built by the Finns with granite from the nearby quarry, at the elevation of the slope of the garden. The shelves of the studio contained relics of the Hales' ancestor Nathan Hale, who was captured by the British as a spy. His last words were the famous, "I regret that I have but one life to give to my country." His water bucket, bearing the name Nathan Hale, and his gun remained on the shelf. Edward Everett Hale's family letters were closeted there, along with letters of family members representing the United States in the Far East.

Folly Cove was the home of many artists: Charles Grafley, Walker Hancock, and George Demetrius, all sculptors, and Leon Kroll, a painter. Further down the road lived Paul Manship. Sculptors were drawn to the area because of the rocky topography. It was a historic spot.

One day, Gertrude Standwood, who was studying with us, planned a party with Lillian Wescott Hale and Margaret Hoyt. The party was to take place in the Standwood's house, which was the oldest in Folly Cove. Built at the time of the Revolution, the house had the shutters to protect the inhabitants from the arrows of the Indians. The Hales' aunt, who had come on a visit from Savannah, Georgia, was also involved in the party plans. As she was a lovely, distinguished-looking lady, William did some etchings of her while she sewed or embroidered. This party was arranged as a celebration of the elderberry wine they had just made. They wanted to enjoy and share the results of their efforts. The impressive array of guests included Mr. Burnham, the Hales, Elizabeth Cummins, Margaret Hoyt, who had been a pupil of Gabrielle Clemens but was now studying etching with us, and the oldest of her three sons. I put them all in a large canvas called *The New England Women,* which Professor James O'Gorman acquired when he bought William's large painting *Artists of Gloucester.*

William experimented with etchings in color throughout that summer. He felt that this was a unique opportunity since he had the studio and the press at his disposal. He was trying to gain certain effects with color by superimposing one color over another on one plate, or with two plates, or in three printings, according to his design. He managed to get an emotional effect in a medium that was so unyielding. As a starting point, he worked the Chevreul colors of the spectrum. It was a combination of rainbow colors and primaries.

With the sea in front of him and the sunrise greeting him, there was an aura of Northern Lights in the morning. When William saw the fishermen lifting their nets not far from our door, he began to work, just as they did. Several standing in one boat, several in the other, gently, gradually, the fishermen pulled the net through the water, as it bobbed at the edges, held up by buoys. They hauled them higher and higher. The boats came closer until the struggling fish were lifted into the dories. This was done as the first refracted rays of sun glided over the water. William captured this scene in his first etching in color called *Fishermen at Sunrise.*

William then began to work on another motif. The second plate, in contrast to the first, was of an interior, with dark colors of depth and mystery. Called *The Discussion,* it had the quality of an old manuscript, or of a page of the Bible—an ancient tome handed down from generation to generation. It represented customs that abounded since the Bible was written. In Babylon the men probably sat in an old stone *cheder* and discussed the human drama and the Creation. Was it six days? Or, a million years? How did these people in the tiny land of Israel combat their adversaries and the tragedy of the loss of their beloved home, their heritage? How did they not succumb, how did they overcome, and how did they survive the destruction of their monument of morality, the Temple of Solomon? That was *The Discussion.* How were they to elevate themselves after the loss, the events that had changed their lives, to achieve a greater understanding of their involvement with God? As they discussed it, it was Moses who had the understanding of the closeness with the Creator. It was he who provided the link between the unspoken and invisible greatness of the cosmos, and the tiny, human, finite individual.

William was able to achieve that concentration with the three heads—three students of the Bible as they listened to the rabbi, which really means "teacher." They were still learning, composing their thoughts onto a plane much higher than they themselves endured. And they survived the Babylon exile, inspired by a vision to rise above their misfortune.

When William was producing this plate, it was a very warm day in the middle of August. He had been working hard, pulling the spike wheel of the press, and he returned to Gaviotta and ate some cold borscht. Afterwards, he became pale and sank to the floor. I thought he had been poisoned by the acids of the plates so I beat up six eggs and persuaded William to swallow them. He couldn't keep them down. At this moment—luckily—Mrs. Mattson from the Finnish colony came in. I told her to get the doctor. Dr. Rowley was not in, but Dr. Carvell, his young assistant, came. He made William lie down on the couch.

"I think he has appendicitis. We'll get him to the hospital," he said.

"I don't think it's appendicitis," I told him.

"What do you think it is, Mrs. Meyerowitz?"

"I think it's color etching."

Dr. Carvell said, "I never had any experience with that condition." In his opinion it was appendicitis, and he thought we ought to take care of it at once.

"Doctor, I'm not sure whether he should be operated on. How long can we wait?"

"Well, you're taking a big chance, but if you insist, we'll wait until tomorrow," he said.

We put him to bed and the doctor told me to give William cold compresses to his side, and no solid food. The Hales were informed and told me: "If you have any difficulty in the night, we'll be watching. Put a lamp in the window, and we'll come and help."

I sat up all night and put cold compresses on William's side, and in the morning I saw that his coloring was slightly better. The doctor came.

"William, I think you're better. Try some clear chicken soup."

I asked Dr. Carvell what he thought it was.

"I don't know, but I think I made the wrong diagnosis. You might have been closer to the truth, Mrs. Meyerowitz."

I gave Mrs. Mattson some money and told her to get a chicken to make the soup. Mrs. Mattson gave him the clear soup and he gradually recovered. I looked at our table and noticed that the money was still there. I turned to her.

She said, "The Lord provideth. The Lord provideth."

Later I found out that it had been Sunday, and a neighbor had given her a chicken.

One day I was sitting overlooking the view where the first shot of the Revolution was fired on Folly Cove. Before me was the slope of the beach, with its huge rocks and sparkling water. Children on a raft looked like floating butterflies. And right in front of me was a little quarry pool, which William had etched and developed into various juxtapositions of forms and colors in his experiments. These were his first abstracts.

Two children played on the edge of the quarry. They were silhouetted against the earthy orange of the rocks. I looked down to sketch, and when I looked up again—there was only one child there. I walked over to the edge of the hill and saw the other child in the water, face down on a rock. I could not rescue him. I rushed to the beach and by sheer determination was able to signal to the Ronka boys on the raft to come to shore. They were wonderful swimmers and one of them dove in and pulled the little boy out. They laid him on the turf and by taking turns at first aid, they caused the boy to begin to breathe. After that experience, William and I decided that we would no longer be staying at Folly Cove with the threat always before us of the children near the quarry pool.

At the end of the summer we returned to New York with a fine collection. I had paintings, and Bill had the etchings, particularly the beautiful etchings in color that he had created at Folly Cove. We were invited by the Milch Gallery to have a show, which was a great success. People marveled at the etchings of Gloucester, particularly *Fishermen at Sunrise*.

In 1920 our baby girl, Isadora, was born in New York, but she survived only a few months. It was a blow to our happiness when some unwelcome visitor transmitted a germ that produced the pneumonia that caused her death. She was beautiful and everyone loved her. It was an idyllic event that passed into oblivion like Rembrandt's Cornelia. I remember the sunny morning when they carried her away and the crib was dismantled.

In 1921 William had a show at the Corcoran Gallery in Washington, D.C. Ralph Cross Johnson, collector of old masters, took some of the etchings, including *The Discussion*, on condition that if they compared well with his old masters, he would buy them, which, in fact, he did. Mr. Johnson escorted us on a tour of Washington to view the cherry blossoms, and he showed us his priceless collection. Beckoning William aside, he asked for his opinion of a certain portrait of an old man with a beard.

"It's from the school of Leonardo."

Next it was my turn. I had waited outside, but said the same thing.

"I paid Berenson a large fee for that information," bemoaned Johnson.

Johnson's friends included Theodore Roosevelt and Justice Oliver Wendell Holmes. The Rockport Art Association had its first show in 1921 at the Congregational Church, and William was asked by Aldro Hibbard to be on the jury.

5
Our First Trip to Europe, 1922

Our first trip to Europe began in London. Mrs. Murphy of Baltimore had given us a letter to Sir John Wright of the Royal Academy. We went to upper Sloan Square, where a woman in a starched apron opened the door. She ushered us up a flight of steps to the living room, which included a fireplace. The many guests who assembled there spoke of the political scene, the queen, and the weather, while tea was served with crumpets. The host was silent, swaying from toe to heel before the fire, his hands behind his back. We just observed the English visitors. After a polite interval they got up to leave.

It seemed to be time for us to go. We said good-bye to our host, but I added, "You remind me of a character in a book."

His face lit up. "What book?"

"*Buried Alive* by Arnold Bennett."

"I must confess—I am the one he wrote about. Don't go! Stay for high tea."

Sir John was also an etcher. His print room was small and dark but with a very nice press. He was tall and athletic looking with a fine personality once you penetrated the crust of reserve. After tea, he took us on a tour of London, to Piccadilly Circus, and to the theater, where we attended a play by George Bernard Shaw, one of those ultrafashionable, smart-talk comedies. Shaw delineated the English upper-class character.

William wanted to have a Friday night dinner, but the people at the hotel could not give us any information; so with his friends, including Dr. Bobrow, we went into the Tube. William said, "I'll follow a Jewish face." We walked through the train and he stopped in front of a man reading the London *Times*. I said, "Are you sure?" Bill nodded. At Piccadilly Circus the man rushed out and we after him. On Oxford Street he ran and we followed. William caught up with him and asked him if he knew where there was a Jewish restaurant. The man answered, "Why do you think I'm hurrying to Abramson's? Come with me."

Arriving on the Continent, we went to Holland, where we saw *The Night Watch*, by Rembrandt. We visited his home in the Jewish Quarter. It was a large, dark edifice with tiny slats for windows, casting mysterious shafts of light. The synagogue close by is where Rembrandt painted his vision of *The Old Testament* and the series of the Virgin.

Amsterdam was a city of bicycles, canals, and cheese shops. In the park a group of men sat on a bench. One of them came over to us. He bowed low and returned to his position. It was exactly the same pose as in William's etching, *The Philosophers*. The men were solving all the ills of the world.

When we arrived in Berlin, we stayed at a hotel on the Donau near Unter den Linden. There was a parade in progress, with people carrying signs saying, "Nei Wieder Krieg"—No More War—to the tune of Beethoven's *Ninth Symphony*—"All Men Are Brothers." Tremendous inflation was prevalent and everything cost thousands of marks. The money in such large denominations was confusing, but our dollars had a high value so we bought art books. In Kasira's Gallery of Modern Art, a Pissarro—*Le Déjeuner sur l'herbe*—was for sale for less than a thousand dollars. This same scene of a landscape with clothed and nude figures sitting on the ground in the midst of fruits and other food was the subject of many famous painters ever since the time of the Italian master Giorgione. We tried to borrow some money from a collector to buy the painting, but to no avail. Years later that painting sold for over $40,000.

In Vienna we stayed at the Hotel Diana Bad. At the end of the Red Tower Street—Roten Turm Strasse—there were many cafés and hotels. We visited Katarina Steiner, who had been a childhood friend of my father's. She was a businesswoman, who was greatly interested in the fact that I was an artist. Later she was taken prisoner during the Nazi avalanche of hate. The Café Diana Bad was the hotel where the Prince of Wales and Mrs. Wallis Warfield Simpson met.

The American ambassador invited us to the embassy for dinner, where a simple interior with a flowered curtain concealed some desks from the dining area. William had made an etching of the mother of one of the ambassador's secretaries, and they wanted to show us around Vienna. The ambassador told us of doing a favor for a gentleman from Sweden. The ambassador then received a roll of etchings as a gift. When he opened it, a whole array of hefty nude women bathers caught his eye. There was one etching of a couple waltzing. He put that on top and rolled them back, laying the etchings on a basket under his desk. When the ambassador returned from his engagement, the roll was gone. The cleaning man had thrown them out. Later, the ambassador learned that it had been a collection of Anders Zorn's works. The ambassador took us to the Royal Opera to hear *The Bartered Bride*. We sat in the American ambassador's box, next to the Royal box, which was empty.

From Vienna, we traveled to the border on our way to Cracow, Poland. The customs officers insisted that we get off the train at Oderberg to allow them to examine our possessions. Our paintings and books were on the train, which went off without us. We ran along with the train yelling, "Throw them out! Throw them out!" But nothing happened. The whole roll of paintings and the books were gone.

There we were, abandoned at the station. We sat down to debate. Several refugees nearby began to pluck at our sleeves. I took out some chocolates and gave them to the people. After they finished the chocolates, the people returned, this time nearly tearing at our jackets. William gave them a box of crackers and still they persisted. Others joined this group to demand food from us. We took out coins for them. A man appeared, who ordered them all back to their seats. This poverty was the aftermath of World War I.

We asked this man where we could find a hotel nearby, as there was no train until 6 A.M. the next morning. He directed us to the only one, where the room was regal, with handknitted bed covers and curtains, and a royal insignia over the bed. We decided not to sleep in the bed, and sat up in big armchairs until daylight, when we ordered hot milk and cereal. Downstairs there was music, and several people were being thrown out of the hotel. I looked out of the window to see what was going on.

In the morning we were back at the station. We spoke to a man waiting for the train who turned out to be from Brooklyn. We had first-class seats in an upholstered compartment, where the dust rose from the upholstery with every turn of the wheels. So, to the dismay of the conductor, we went into the third-class carriage where there were wooden benches.

In Cracow we visited my aunt, Regina Kahany, who was a musician and had taught piano for many years. Her son, Menachem, was in Geneva working for Chaim Weizmann, who was to become the first president of Israel. My uncle, Joseph Kahany, was head of the railroad, and he received a gold chain for his achievement in management. Both he and his wife were annihilated by the Nazis in 1942.

Cracow was picturesque. It extended from the Vavel Fortress on a hill to the Tuchhalle, an enclosure in the city square, akin to Faneuil Hall in Boston.

We went to the Jewish Quarter where William painted his synagogue scene by hiding behind an iron door. He painted the *bimah,* or pulpit, in the center with a cage of yeshiva *bocher*—schoolboys. The painting of this synagogue is in the collection of Cantor Alec Zimmer in Boston. The nearby park, called the Plantation, ran through the city. William painted a view of the river and the park.

Next we went to Italy.

Florence is a small city with great art treasures packed within its confines. The Arno River runs through the city, and the famous bridge, Ponte Vecchio, crosses the river. Michelangelo and Leonardo da Vinci were apparent everywhere. In the piazza at the center of the city, everyone congregated in the cafés and art galleries. We stayed in a little place called 35 Via de Marmora, the Street of the Academy, where Michelangelo's statues of slaves were exhibited.

Chiara Beccetini was our hostess. We lived in an old palace that had been converted into apartments with high ceilings, decorated with the look of the Renaissance. The spacious stairways were made of iron, but the walls, halls, and floors were marble.

Close by was the Piazza Signoria, where the great sculpture of *David* by Michelangelo stands in a rather shadowy corner. It was impressive and both William and I made drawings of it.

Returning to our apartment on the *secunda piana*—second floor—Chiara Beccetini always had supper ready for us. Then William would take out the zither and sing Italian songs. Chiara, with her boyfriend and other young friends, would sit around the table and listen to him.

Dostoevski had once lived in Florence, and we found a building with his name on the door. The Brownings had also lived in Florence. We saw the beautiful little park and the old church where the magnificent statues of *Night* and *Day* by Michelangelo were exhibited.

We met Mrs. Cantara, who owned a small hotel in Venice, although she was staying in Florence. She took us to meet her friend, Schmulovitz, the tailor, who reminded us of Figaro from the Rossini opera, *The Barber of Seville.* He was able to accomplish all sorts of tasks and to meet everyone's needs. He exchanged money for us and told us where to buy what and how to go where to see what we wanted to find. They brought William to a little synagogue on an old street, where a service was being held. The women sat up in the balcony. After the service the congregants asked William to say a few words in Hebrew. They handed him a book and he went up to the *bimah* and began to sing in the cantorial manner that was so melodic, soft and soothing. The men were excited and grasped him on both shoulders and said, "You must not leave Florence. You've got to stay here."

He said, "I'm going to be here another week."

"No. You must stay here. We'll give you a position in our synagogue as the cantor."

The women also loved his singing. They descended from their balcony and implored him to stay. "Can't you take one year from your life and spend it with us?"

William answered, "That would be beautiful, but I have other plans. Anyway, I'll sing for you again while I'm here."

There was a small shop in Florence, and William saw a lovely cameo. I liked it very much, and Bill bought it for me as a memento of our visit.

We next took a bus to Assisi in order to see the marvelous murals by Giotto, the primitive, shining example of an early Italian master. There is a legend that Giotto was a young shepherd and as he tended the sheep with their round backs, he drew the animals with a sharpened stone on a rock. The great artist Cimabue happened to be passing by on a donkey, and when he saw Giotto's drawing, he said, "I must take this boy to the studio and teach him to be an artist."

In time, Giotto became known for his beautiful curved line. When Pope Julius was inquiring for someone to make the mural in the church at Assisi, he was given a drawing consisting of only a circle. He was told that this was an example of Giotto's work.

The Pope said, "He is the artist who will do the mural in the cathedral of Assisi."

We stayed at a hotel that was very busy at lunchtime because tourists ate there. They would look at the cathedral, the museums, and the marketplace, and then depart. But we remained. The furniture in the hotel was new, including the tables and chairs. The staircase, though, was very old and beautiful. We had an exceptional view of the plains going off in the direction of Bologna. Near us was an old town gate that probably had been there since the tenth or eleventh century. We both made sketches of it.

The next day we took a taxi that had two doors which opened, allowing the passenger to step in, like a baby carriage. We were taken all the way up, high onto the mountain where St. Francis had spoken to the birds.

On the way to Venice we took a train with several travelers in our compartment. William asked them about hotels, and they gave him a few addresses. They said we were on the wrong coach, that we had to go forward to get the train to Venice. They ushered me into an empty compartment. I heard the door closing behind me, but I dug my nails into the hand on the door. I started yelling, "Help! Police!" William was still in the corridor, holding his suitcase. The men had tried to steal his passport, but we foiled their attempt, and they ran away. In the adjoining compartment, we spoke to a man from the American Embassy. He advised us to go to the Hotel Europa with him. The moment we arrived, friends from Hartford, Connecticut, greeted us and said, "Tomorrow we will show you Venice."

The next morning I was waiting for William on a bench in front of the hotel, facing a small canal bridge. No one was about. Suddenly, two men approached, one with a bandaged face. I stood up and began shouting, "Help, Police!" They fled and I realized they were the same men who had tried to steal William's passport.

William worked outdoors in Venice with his etching plate. It was of copper covered with a wax ground. As he was etching, two little boys were watching from a railing. One said to the other, *"pointe d'oro,"* which means he was working with a needle of gold. The line of the copper glistened in the sun.

Owing to the favorable rate of exchange, our plan to stay in Europe for three months was stretched to five. We had left money with the Cunard Line Office in order to be sure that we would have enough to return to the United States. When we got back to Paris we found that "Voluta," as it was called, had increased still more, and the money we had saved for the second-class trip home was now converted, and we had a cabin right at the end, where we would be first-class passengers.

Our wardrobe consisted of only basics so we decided we should try to find some clothes to make ourselves look as if we belonged in first class.

Wandering around the shops of Paris, hoping to find some elegant looking clothes, we passed the Magasin de Louvre, a department store, where the mannequins in the window wore just the kind of fashions we wanted. There was a lovely gown of white chiffon with black sequins in Grecian style, and the male mannequin on the other side of the window was dressed in an evening suit. We entered the store and sought out the manager. William explained to him, in French, that we were artists. He sold us the complete outfits for what we could afford.

We boarded the boat—I think it was the *Mauritania,* an English Cunard liner—and found ourselves in the first-class section where everybody dressed each night for dinner. We donned our evening clothes, and the head steward said, "You're going to sit at the table with another couple," who were from Rochester, New York. The second night out, the waiter gave us a menu and we had become the hosts. After dinner, Bill and I had a consultation. "This means we have to give him a tip," which we didn't have. The couple said, "Well, we'll have to figure out something." They confessed that they were on their first trip to Europe, and did not know the right thing to do. In addition, the waiter at our table was the head waiter of the second class.

We had a rough night. The orchestra was playing, but half the time the bows played by the cellists and violinists didn't strike the instruments. There was a pause, and then, finally, the music would continue as the boat would rock back into balance, and the dishes on the table would slide from side to side. There were wooden edges around each table to keep the dishes from flying on the floor.

The next night was very calm, and we had a beautiful still life in the center of our table, which looked like one of William's paintings. It consisted of a tier of fruit, then flowers, and on top were roses. We had everything from soup to Baked Alaska for dessert. Mr. Finecune from Rochester said to William, "The artistic dinner has given us great pleasure."

One of the guests on the ship was Leon Bakst, the great designer for Sergei Diaghilev of the Ballet Russe. Soon William and he were chatting away in French and in Russian and having a good time. Suddenly Bakst got seasick. I had to feed him in order to bring him back to himself. He was a congenial and outgoing person with sandy hair. He told us a lot about the directors of the ballet and about the dancers. He described their idiosyncrasies and how they struggled to achieve their artistic perfection.

And so our first trip abroad ended. It was one of the most exciting adventures of our early years together.

6
Gloucester, 1923

We came back to East Gloucester and stayed in Mr. Little's house on the corner of Rocky Neck Avenue and Eastern Point Road. There was still a trolley line to the city on Main Street, which went to the end of Rocky Neck Avenue where a grocery store stood. Further on, at the end of the Neck, was a shipyard for the repair of fishing boats. There was a large red brick chimney, which can be seen in some of William's early harbor etchings. He did this scene from the high cliffs overlooking Main Street. We were then exhibiting at the Gallery on the Moors near Ledge Road.

During the summer of 1923 we had the top floor apartment, consisting of two rooms, which we shared with Mr. and Mrs. Peter Neagoe. Peter was a Rumanian who had been a school chum of William's at the National Academy of Design. William painted his portrait. Peter's wife studied sculpture, but she shifted to painting. Peter turned to writing. They had been in Paris, and she always spoke of their friend Picasso.

Stuart Davis was downstairs with his brother, Wyatt, and their mother and father. The house had a big porch where we used to sketch and do views of Rocky Neck and "Norman's Woe," where Longfellow wrote his poem, *The Wreck of the Hesperus*, which William etched.

Abraham Haddad, a rug dealer, resided on the main floor. He frequently served us café expresso with sweet syrup. He and William used to sing songs together in Hebrew and Arabic. He taught us a lot about Oriental rugs.

Next door to us lived Romney Marie, a famous bohemian of the Greenwich Village of the 1920s. She ran a Village Tea Room in Gloucester where artists congregated, trying to find patronage in a world that was not thinking about art. Potential buyers always said, "Well, we'll think about it." The artists sat and waited.

We often went up the hill of Mount Pleasant Avenue, taking our canvases, easels, and paintboxes. In those days the route was little more than a cow path, and we frequently encountered a colorful native, Orin Parsons, leading his cows to pasture. When we reached the top we had a magnificent view of Gloucester, its wharves, the shore line, and church steeples. There was an old house at the very top. We would knock on the door and ask for water to wash our brushes.

One day the lady of the house said, "You are always up here painting. Why don't you save the trouble of walking and buy my home? My children are married and I want to live near them."

As we were descending the hill, a car stopped. The driver, a distinguished looking man, offered us a ride.

"I am Judge Brumback. Do you recall, we met at the Atwoods'? My wife is also an artist, and she admires your work. May I bring her to see you?"

The next morning the Brumbacks visited us and selected several of William's etchings. Then the judge said, "Get into the car. We'll go to the bank and find out about the house." He had overheard our conversation.

He took us to the Cape Ann Bank and introduced us to his friend Roger Babson, the president of the bank, who produced a document.

"Will you please sign this, Mr. and Mrs. Meyerowitz, for your house."

We signed and they congratulated us on our acquisition. As we walked out on Main Street, I said to William, "We own property." He felt a tap on his shoulder. Roger Babson had run after him.

"We forgot to ask you for a deposit."

We had a quick consultation and paid $40 for the down payment. We moved into our new house in 1924.

We grew to love this house, and William's passion for it resulted, oddly enough, in one of his first forays into the field of abstract art. He decided to fix and repaint the floors, which were old and shabby. In the kitchen he painted imitation inlaid linoleum. For the living room, he made a triangular design on a yellow ground. It was so modern for that time, that it could have graced the walls of the Museum of Modern Art. A collector came in to see our paintings. We showed him landscapes from the hill, and paintings of musicians and of horses. But he kept looking at the floor. Finally he said, "I would like to buy this floor."

"We don't want to sell our floor. How could we manage?"

"Don't worry. I'll have my man saw it out and bring you another set of boards, and we'll put another floor down for you."

"What would happen to the furniture?" I asked. "The whole house would collapse while we're waiting for a new floor."

"Well, think about it," he said. "I'll be back in two weeks."

I went to Boston to do some shopping. At the Morgan Memorial, I bought a second-hand rug and we covered the living room floor with it. When the collector returned, we kept the floor concealed so as not to remind him of his outlandish desire. He confined himself to looking at our paintings, forgetting about his earlier request.

Our neighbor Stuart Davis suggested whimsically, "I think we ought to get William to pose against his floor."

Stuart and his brother Wyatt, who was a photographer, laid Bill right across the floor, and they stood on a big table. Wyatt photographed William lying on the floor as if he were resting against a wall.

The basement was the ground, with a few rocks. Mr. Pomeroy, the mason, came over and removed the big rock from the lower basement so that we would have more room for a studio. William decided that he would like to have a floor there, and they put down cement. William said, "I'd like that floor to be Indian red."

"That would take tons of red powder," Mr. Pomeroy said.

Albert Einstein after lecture at New York University 1923

But William said, "No, I think if you just leave the cement wet, we can pounce the powder on the top and it will look like a red floor."

They tried it and it worked. Mr. Pomeroy made red floors for other people using that method.

To make a little more room, William took out the old furnace that was cracked. Then he built a wall to divide the basement into two parts, one for all the necessities and the other for painting. He made a floor out of boxes that he took apart and laid down, and it was very effective.

Since the chimney went all the way down to the basement, William decided to build a fireplace there. One of our pupils, Maurice Stephens, was an antique dealer in Essex.

He brought bricks from an Essex house over a hundred years old, from which they constructed a beautiful fireplace. It looked as if it had always been at that very spot. The angle was just right—$33\frac{1}{3}°$—so the fire would go up the chimney and no smoke would remain in the lower studio. William built a shelf under the window for his pupils to put their plates and paints on, which gave a desklike appearance. The students could also go out in the garden and work on the old bench that had belonged to Captain Foster. His wife gave it to us as a present because we always sat on it in her garden when we were painting the harbor. Although the bench was battered, the long, fluted design, with all the little edgings of the antique Lower Colonial style, could still be seen. Every pupil sat on that bench and painted.

Bill took the stairway that ran down the back of the house to use in the garden. He painted a picture of me sitting before the Franklin stove in the dining room. John Pomeroy had given us the stove in 1925. William had restored the parts and put it into the wall with asbestos backing. It was a metal stove of the type invented by Benjamin Franklin. After William refurbished it, John Pomeroy said, "I want to buy the stove for a client." I said, "I'll find you another." And I did find one in Boston.

William often worked on the house while I would take an afternoon nap. On one such occasion, I heard the sound of sawing at the back of the house, in the lower studio. When I went downstairs, I saw that William had cut a window space between the two windows of the lower basement. He added the third window almost identical to the Washington Arms originals. Afterwards, there was plenty of light for painting in the basement.

When we had moved into our house, I looked at the rafters, which were black. Then I remembered that George Stacey, the proprietor of the Hawthorne Inn, had told us one evening that he had built a house on top of a hill for his assistant, using the remnants of the Washington Arms, which had been the first inn of Gloucester. It had burned down. Seeing that the rafters of our house were heavily blackened with soot, I surmised that this was the house he meant.

I was curious about the origin of the name, "Washington Arms" for the inn, as well as "Washington Street" in Gloucester. I believe that boats for the Continental Army had been built at Marblehead, then brought to New Jersey for the army to go across the Delaware River and overpower the Hessians. From Massachusetts, the boats would not have gone empty. In the dead of the winter, they would certainly have taken fish because that was what Gloucester was famous for. Fish was the only food that could be found and that could have been preserved in the cold. The fish would have enabled the soldiers to survive. George Washington may have come to Gloucester later, to thank the fishermen. It is also possible that Washington would have visited this place, at least once, and even in secret, since it was the closest point to England.

When we were having the house painted, William told the workman, "Be sure to clear out the areas on top, where the drain pipes are." Bill devised a long pole with a mirror on the end, like a dentist's mirror for examining the teeth at the back of the mouth. He lowered it out of the skylight in the attic and found that the whole pipe was full of leaves. He called the painter and repeated, "Clean out the water pipe." The man insisted that he had done it. William said, "You didn't, and I'll show you how I know." The man just couldn't believe it, and, of course, he cleared out the pipes after that.

William was always fixing, building, and restoring the house and its contents. He upholstered all the chairs at one time or another. We found antique furniture in many places. Some genuine family heirlooms from my childhood home in Philadelphia included a Tiffany lamp of metal with colored glass inlay. On the four shelves in the alcove by the stove, there was some china that belonged to my grandmother.

Among the things that William fixed was a chair that had been too high. He lowered the seat so that it was like a little step. He covered it with a lovely cloth, and then we would show our paintings on it. The back was high and it would accommodate a painting as big as forty inches.

Sometimes, people would say, "Is this painting for sale?" He would say, "No." "We're interested in buying it." His retort was, "It's not for sale, but it's for buying." In other words, if you want to buy it, it can be arranged.

Mr. Pimpstein often called and said he wanted to buy a painting. He always came to look at William's work and said, "I'll think about it." When he would return, the painting would be gone, and he would fret. One day Mr. Pimpstein made up his mind that he wanted a particular painting. He went away, then telephoned and said,

"Do you think it will fit on a fourteen-foot wall?"

"Yes."

"I don't know what to do. My wife gets very upset when something new is brought in."

Mr. Pimpstein bought the painting anyway, and hung it in his office. When his wife saw it, she liked it and wanted it in the house.

We always prepared our own canvases. We would buy a large roll of linen and put it on the refectory table, and use it as a tablecloth. I would say to my guests, "Don't spill any soup or butter on the tablecloth."

They said, "Since when are you so fussy?"

But every time we needed some canvas, we would cut off a piece, and the tablecloth became shorter and shorter.

One day a friend remarked, "I can't understand why this tablecloth keeps shrinking all the time."

We had to confess that it was no longer a tablecloth, but rather, it was now in our collection of recent paintings.

When it came to restoring paintings, Bill was equally adroit. He was able to take a painting that was not quite the size of the stretcher and add another piece of canvas of the same quality. He would get some carpenter's glue, cook it, and use part of it. Or he might use wallpaper paste, which was also very adhesive. He would spread the glue or the paste on the piece of linen, large enough to cover a little more than the space he needed. Then he would put the piece of linen under a weight. Next, he would add the painting to the stretched edge in such a way that it hardly ever showed. He knew how to do this because he had learned to retouch old photographs when as a boy he had assisted the photographer in Russia.

He was also able to increase the size of a stretcher. He would add about two inches by putting some wooden slabs on the edge and then add another strip—what is called a two-inch strip—on top of the slabs. Then the canvas could be stretched if it was larger, on a stretcher that was maybe eighteen or twenty-two inches. William was skillful at doing this. I never saw any other artist increase the size of his stretchers. If William had a piece of canvas that was an odd size, he would immediately make an appropriate stretcher.

He liked to make triangles with the stretchers, or to do round paintings. One time he did a round painting of dancers. Then the question was, "Where will we get a circular frame?" We were taking a walk when a young man approached us, carrying a round frame, which we induced him to sell to us. It was like a gift, dropped from the skies, and was exactly the right size for the painting.

With three basic shapes—the square, the circle, and the triangle—William was able to find new forms of expression. He began his experiments in abstract art in 1920. One painting of dancers was mostly lines and spaces in various directions. A musical canvas was completely abstract. Many drawings were on the verge of the nonobjective, although they still had all the essence of nature. An advanced thinker, William was doing this before it became the norm for other artists.

On the windows, William put up large boards with hinges so they could be opened or shut to get more or less light. The lights needed to be adjusted on the western windows. The two north windows gave us a perfect studio light. When the sun was going down in the late afternoon, we opened the western windows and there was a great deal of light in the studio.

In the autumn evenings, we used to take a little table from the studio and place it in front of the fireplace. William would split some logs and light the fire. We watched the images in the embers. We would feast on a simple meal. Sometimes we burned newspaper clippings that had been stories printed about us, and it was like a scene from *La Bohème*. We would have cozy conversations about our work, our friends, ourselves, and they were precious evenings we spent together. We never tired of each other's company. It was always interesting. From the day we met, our life was one absorbing conversation.

We talked of how my father had been one of the first to produce artificial silk in this country in 1910. At that time, Japan was overpowering the United States with its silk industry. My father, Isadore Bernstein, along with his brother, Henry, created a facsimile with textiles before the rayon era.

I probably inherited some of my feeling for color and design from my father. William felt that he had inherited his artistic ability from his grandfather, whose beautiful designs drawn on vellum were put in *mezzuzas*, the small containers of the holy word that are found on doorways in Jewish homes.

William said he had learned how to row a boat by imitating the older boys at his grandfather's place by the river. He always loved water and boats. In New York City, William often went to Central Park to row on the lake. Bill used to paint the still water, catching the reflections in the depths and the sky on the surface. The Duck Pond in Gloucester attracted him because it was a freshwater retreat right near the ocean.

Having a garden was wonderful for him. He planted all around the property, and took away many maple shoots that would have suffocated the other growing things. He planted lilac bushes, day lilies, and the orange lilies that would open and be in their glory just around the beginning of July, and which I therefore called Fourth of July lilies. The day lilies were very white and fragrant, but they didn't last long. At night, most of the flowers, especially the lilies, would close their leaves in order to shelter their hearts, the apex of their beauty.

William planted grass by prodding the ground with a plank imbedded with nails. He would add some sod to make the ground more even. Eventually he achieved the goal of a real garden, which he called his paradise. I wondered if Monet had raised his water lilies, or if Van Gogh raised his sunflowers, or whether Cézanne had raised his apples. William and I often made paintings of each other in the garden.

William planted a little pear tree that grew until it was like an umbrella over the garden table. The tree grew so high that it obscured our view from the window, and had to be trimmed. The tree cutter protested, saying, "If you trim it, the tree will never grow anymore."

But the tree said, "If William Meyerowitz planted me, I'll become the biggest pear tree of all."

The tree keeps greening and growing every year. It is still yielding treasure.

MAKING WINE

The grapevine trail was a branch from the vine in Mike's garden. It crawled through the fence on our side and William quickly attached it to the peach tree that was on the wane. He made a pretty festoon, almost like a little arbor. Soon we began to have concord grapes, which William gathered for wine. We sterilized bottles with boiling water. He filled a big bowl with water and put the grapes in it. We pinched each grape and threw them into the bottles. When he had a layer of grapes, William added a layer of sugar. Another layer of grapes, and another of sugar, followed. When the bottle was about half filled, William took some cotton wadding and put it into the neck of the bottle. Then he tied a piece of cheesecloth around the top. The row of bottles stood on a shelf for about three or four weeks. Every once in a while he would test them to see if the wine was beginning to ferment. When the wine was almost ready, he took another bottle with a wide neck, put cheesecloth over the top, and poured the juice from the first bottle into the second, restraining the grapes. All of the bottles were treated like this. He would examine the color against the light. Soon the grapes took on a beautiful burgundy shade, the blue turned to red, and red turned into purple. And it was wine.

One evening, about six o'clock, as we sat in the dining room eating, there was a great explosion! We looked at each other. William said, "Get under the table, quick!" We both slid off our chairs and waited under the table for something to happen. But that was all. We crawled out and went to see what it was all about. There was no apparent damage anywhere. Finally he began to have some inkling. He opened the closet where the wine bottles were stored. Someone had put a cork into the wine bottles. No doubt, it had been one of our pupils. The bottle had exploded because wine has to be left open while it is fermenting; it cannot be corked. All the damage was in the closet.

In the fall, we finished up in the garden, cutting down peony bushes and leaving the shasta daisies that Bill had planted outside the three windows of the lower studio. We kept pulling out the young maple trees that grew profusely. Quantities of peaches and pears were gathered for our harvest.

Whatever he planted became the motive of his art.

7

The Whitney Studio Club—The Art Scene

THE ART SCENE IN NEW YORK WAS VERY EXCITING IN THE 1920s, AND WILLIAM AND I WERE actively involved in it. We were invited members of the Whitney Studio Club. Mrs. Gertrude Whitney was a patron of the arts, and a fine sculptress as well. She had designed a monument in memory of those lost on the *Titanic* when it struck an iceberg and sank in April 1912 on its maiden voyage. Mr. and Mrs. Isadore Strauss of the Macy's department store fortune and two of Mrs. Whitney's closest friends had been among the victims. Mrs. Whitney's monument, which she exhibited along with the paintings of members of the Whitney Studio Club, was a figure of a drowning nude woman.

Mrs. Whitney held a masquerade ball in her Museum on Eighth Street, on which occasion the artists of the Studio were treated to a collation. Waiters in evening clothes and starched shirts circulated, carrying trays of food.

Each artist was supposed to design his or her own costume. Since William loved horses, he decided to go as a French cab driver. He put on a high hat and I sewed cuffs on his shoes, and he took a white duck coat and decorated it. In the lapel he painted a big sunflower. In one pocket he had a large bottle of French wine, in the other, he had Virginia stogies. On the back he made a Cézanne still life with apples rolling off a very crooked table. From his belt hung all his gadgets, his keys, gloves, and pipe. He carried a large, flexible whip and pulled the end down into a loop and tied it with a yellow ribbon.

For me, he designed a wire base for a hat to represent the crown of Catherine the Great. I crocheted bands around the hat and embellished them with beads of various colors to make them shimmer like the crown jewels of Russia. I wore a long cape with green edges over my evening gown.

Our friend Reginald Marsh came as a lifeguard. He had reddish hair and a tan complexion and he looked like he had been out in the sun all day watching over bathers. Peggy Bacon came as a lady suffragette. Mrs. Force, the director of the Whitney Gallery, who had red hair, had dyed it a carrot color. It came down to her shoulders and with her green eyes and green skirt that flopped as she walked, she seemed a vivid impersonation of Rudyard Kipling's "A Rag, a Bone and a Hank of Hair."

Reggie Marsh and I were dancing a waltz, and William had been dancing with Peggy. He was relaxing on a high-backed old chair that was in the hall when Mrs. Julianna Force came in, sat on his lap, put her arms around his shoulders, and said, "Kiss me, kiss me."

William looked at her and said, "You're not my cup of tea."

She got off.

Isadora Duncan came dressed as a Greek dancer with sandals on her feet. She was small and mobile, like a Gaston Lachaise sculpture. And Lachaise came carrying a lyre, representing the poet Homer, with a crown of leaves encircling his head. Bill Zorach arrived as the sculptor he actually was, carrying a tool in his hand. Joseph Stella came as the "Fat Man," which he was, and Heywood Broun, the journalist, not to be outdone, appeared as his corpulent self. Heywood always sat on two chairs. Once when we were attending an artists' meeting at Town Hall, Heywood happened to be sitting in front of me. His chair was so narrow that I shoved another chair under him.

Mrs. Whitney was clad in a long black chiffon gown glittering with gold sequins. She looked very stately. A young artist who had just had his first exhibition there flung his arms around her neck and said, "Ah, you are so wonderful to give this party, you're the greatest patron of the arts that New York ever had, and I'm so happy that I'm here at this party. I want to thank you in person."

Mrs. Whitney had just introduced William and me to the Spanish ambassador who was standing on her left. She looked at us in despair, and we grabbed the arms of the young artist and pulled him away from her. She was thin and the young man was strong and vigorous, in the flush of youth, and something more.

Finally wrenched from the embrace, the young man backed up slowly, falling down the steps one by one, landing at the base, full length on the floor. But the waiters disdainfully passed around him with their silver trays; they never bothered to pick him up, and he lay there fast asleep.

Another eccentric celebrant was Childe Hassam, a tall, gaunt painter with a sun-burned visage and iron gray hair that curled in massive waves over his forehead. He was a heavy drinker and he hadn't been at the party very long when he tottered into the hall with the intention of reclining on a chaise longue, but he rolled off and slumped underneath it, snoring loudly. Nearby was a container filled with pink-speckled lilies. I went over and picked up a spray and laid it on Childe's shirt.

Not only young artists gathered at the Whitney Studio Club. Actors such as John and Lionel Barrymore, and composers and lyricists like George and Ira Gershwin would mingle with painters to discuss the universal problems of the arts. Some of the artists who attended were not well off. Guy Pene Du Bois, a friend of ours who painted high-society women, had to take up art criticism as a means of earning a livelihood. Artists like Stuart Davis did cartoons for the *Masses,* a magazine of social content.

John Sloan, who continually railed against a nation that neglected its artists, helped to found the Society of Independent Artists, for which Mrs. Whitney provided some backing. William and I became charter members of the society. William was elected treasurer, but there wasn't much treasure to spend. Walter Pach was another founder of the Independent Artists, and A. Baylenson was the secretary.

In an effort to show the work of its members, the society put their paintings on exhibition at the old Astor Hotel on Broadway and Forty-fifth Street, where the paintings were hung alphabetically by the artists' names. Salvadore Dali sent an entry called

The Fountain. It was a new toilet and represented his "ready-made" objects, which the society decided to include. Shahn and Robert Henri were represented in the show, as was William, with a large painting of the *Crucifixion.* Unfortunately, there was a strike of elevator operators the night the exhibition opened and we had to walk up eight flights of steps to attend the ceremonies.

Members of the Independent Artists were a varied group. George Bellows, who looked like a baseball player, was talented. He had first gained recognition by his paintings and lithographs of wrestlers. Another member and a good friend of ours was John Sloan, who, incredible as it may seem, didn't actually sell a painting until he was sixty years old. He did, however, sell etchings before that age, and I bought one myself, *The Barber Shop.* He was there with his wife Dolly, who was diminutive but very dynamic. Our friend Edward Hopper attended the opening with his wife, Josephine, who was also an artist. Josephine complained that she was not recognized and was overshadowed by her husband. I advised her to change her name.

Many artists joined the Society of Independent Artists to share our concern for the plight of the painter in a materialistic society that was insensitive to artistic dissent and innovation.

In addition to the artists we knew in New York, artists who visited Gloucester would come to our home, and we would introduce them to the other members of the art colony. One visitor was Edward Hopper, who was very tall, and drove a car that was so small that he had to jack-knife himself to get into it in order to drive. He would marvel that we did so much of our painting outdoors.

"I can only paint in the studio," he confessed. "I make my drawings outdoors and then I take the material inside and try to visualize the scene."

Milton Avery was a spontaneous artist with a fascinating quality to his work. Still another friend was David Burluik, who painted farm scenes of his native Russia. David was an eccentric who wore a spoon in his lapel to indicate that he would accept an invitation. And there was Umberto Romano, a powerful painter; Peter Blume, whose painting *South of Scranton* became a major tour de force; and Raphael Soyer, who visited us frequently.

One artist who became an especially cherished friend was Marcel Duchamp, creator of the celebrated painting *Nude Descending a Staircase.* Actually, there was neither a nude nor a staircase in the painting, but a series of flat tones contrasting against one another in a sort of broken card effect. This work created a sensation in the art world in the history-making Armory exhibition that took place in New York in 1913 and featured the early paintings of Matisse and Picasso. We first met Marcel when he came to one of William's exhibitions. Marcel was an intellectual and a fascinating conversationalist. He would spend a whole day sitting and talking with William. It was too bad that we didn't have a tape recorder in those days. In the mid-forties, Marcel examined a painting of William's of a violinist. Actually, the painting was a composite of three famous musicians whom William had studied—Jascha Heifetz, Isaac Stern, and Mischa Elman. He knew their very gesture, the way they held their bows and fingered the strings.

Marcel said, "You know, I think William Meyerowitz is the Debussy of American art. His art is like Debussy's sunken cathedral; it's below the surface, but you can feel that it's there and that it's whispering to you."

Marcel and William used to play chess together for hours on end. Once, the French painter observed, "My work is influenced by the game of chess. The king, the queen, and the pawns are symbols of the human race; the castle is the fortress of war; the horse represents conquest for peace and progress."

Our circle of friends was not confined to artists. Through our introduction to collectors, we were also friendly with people who were in the world of business and finance. Nat and Belle Lenert were among these friends. She was a decorator; he was an accountant.

In the 1920s, we became close to Benjamin Graham, an influential stockbroker who was active during the stockmarket boom in Wall Street that preceded the historic crash of 1929. Through Graham and his wife, Hazel, we also met David Sarnoff, the head of RCA, and his charming wife, Lissette. The Grahams and the Sarnoffs were admirers of William's work. Sarnoff particularly appreciated his etchings. We were frequently invited to parties the Sarnoffs gave during the carefree, halcyon days of the 1920s.

David Sarnoff had a pleasant singing voice, and he and William, to the delight of the guests, sang songs about their native Russia, including the Volga River Boatmen's Ditty, and "Stenka Rosen," the Cossack love song. Frequently Sarnoff and Graham discussed the free-swinging, wheeler-dealers of Wall Street, who "cornered the market" and made fortunes from their manipulations. The stock of David Sarnoff's own corporation became the victim of an attempted "corner" just before the big market crash. Graham had a fabulous sense of the worth of stocks and bonds, and he wrote a book that became the bible for Wall Street investors.

We were invited to dinner at the Ritz Carlton by Mr. Uris, the real estate operator. We were way up in the ballroom overlooking the city. He showed William the Barbizon Plaza and the Buckingham and he said, "I own these also." Then William said, "Look at all of Central Park and the Palisades. I own all of that." William was referring to the etchings and paintings he had made of those places. Mr. Uris gave William the key to the ballroom so he could go there to sketch any time it suited him. And that is where William made the rare etchings of skyscrapers.

One of the people who appreciated these etchings was Mayor Fiorello La Guardia. William used to say about New York, "It's like any other city—up to the thirtieth floor. Then it becomes New York." When one of William's skyscraper etchings was exhibited at a municipal show, Mayor La Guardia saw it, snatched it from the wall, and purchased it to hang in his office. On another occasion, a mural that had been commissioned during the WPA era was acquired by La Guardia, and hung on his wall in City Hall. In this mural William had depicted the lights and theater of Broadway at night, as well as construction activities.

Some of William's collectors were eccentric. Dr. Isadore Shapiro, who had an odd way of buying art, would hold the painting upside down; if he liked the composition he would throw water at it and mutter, "Well, it's practically damaged goods now. What do you want for it?"

One of our earliest collectors was Leon Huhner, a lawyer who asked William to paint his portrait. Leon introduced William to the Judeans—a society of Jewish intellectuals. We attended meetings of the society that were hosted by Lord Reading of England, who represented an analogous society in Britain, called the Maccabees. Jacob Schiff, the eminent banker and philanthropist, was a fellow Judean. Once, Schiff came to an exhibit at a settlement house where he saw an etching of a rabbi that William had done. Schiff took the etching off the wall, but a young lady in charge of the exhibition stopped him.

"Pardon me, you can't do that."

The banker took out his card, handed it to her, and said, "I'll take care of the price."

One morning in 1929 William was etching in Central Park near the bridle path when a rider on a horse stopped. "I want to pose for you." He was Maurice, the celebrated designer of the house of Schiapparelli in Paris. William made a picture of Maurice. Thereafter, my suits and coats were designed by Maurice in exchange for our work.

One memorable dinner party in which we were active, if unexpected, participants, was given by our friends, Rina and Alec Lieberman, in Merion, Pennsylvania. Their cook left suddenly before the guests arrived. We happened to be there as weekend guests. Rina turned desperately to us.

"What shall I do?"

"Don't worry. Let's call a delicatessen," William suggested.

We ordered a turkey, had it sliced, and put together a meal, with all the trimmings, the salads, and the apple pie. The Liebermans had a governess for their children, and we enlisted her as a waitress for the occasion, dressing her in a long smock with a red bandana taken from the children's room. We polished a large Duncan Phyfe table and set the glassware which sparkled with rare beauty, down to the last brandy tumbler. William arranged a bowl of fruit in the center flanked by yellow lilies from the greenhouse, as meticulously as if he were painting one of his still lifes. The guests included Leopold Stokowski, the conductor, and members of the Philadelphia Orchestra, as well as the artist, Jules Pascin, and Gaston Lachaise. William suggested that after dinner, in a whimsical reversal of roles, all the musicians should make sketches and the artists should perform musical numbers.

The festivities took place in most charming surroundings. The Liebermans' mezzanine was a gallery of French Impressionist paintings and their large living room contained additional works by Renoir, Modigliani, Utrillo, and Derain. William sang a hunting song in French and a series of early Italian seventeenth-century pieces. I put on a ballet costume and did a little dance.

Dr. Clarabel Cone and Eta Cone were sisters whom we met in Baltimore in 1930 when we were invited to exhibit at the Baltimore Museum of Art. The sisters visited the museum and left word that we should return the visit to them at their home in Eutaw Place to see their own collection of paintings. They requested us to bring some of our work for them to view. Their apartment was actually two suites connected together, crammed to the ceiling with a number of paintings by Matisse and Picasso and several landscapes by Cézanne and other French Impressionists. As we showed our work, Eta said, "I like Mr. Meyerowitz's Central Park scene very much. How much is it?" William told her. Just then the telephone rang and she left the room to take the call. Clarabel immediately sat down at the desk and wrote out a check.

"All right, I'll take it."

When Eta returned, she announced, "I like the work very much and I will give you a check for it."

"Thanks," William answered, "But your sister has already taken care of it."

Eta gave her sister an angry look. "You sneak."

It turned out that each of the sisters had her own collection, and they were intensely competitive. Eta looked at other works of William's and finally settled for a watercolor of a still life and a colored etching of Central Park. Clarabel selected a beach scene of mine.

In Clarabel's apartment there was a large blue nude by Matisse, in a hand-carved gold frame, hung, of all places, over a bathtub.

"Aren't you afraid that when you take a hot bath, the steam will spoil the painting?" I asked.

"On the contrary," she replied, "It's very good for oil paintings to have moisture. It keeps them from drying up."

I asked if any specks of paint ever fell into the bathtub.

"No, it's holding up very well."

I would have been afraid to take a bath in that tub for fear the painting would slip off the wall. It was at least five-and-a-half feet long and it was hung with a thin piece of wire. It was called *The Blue Nude*.

In the living room, Clarabel had a large portrait of her cousin Gertrude Stein, done by Matisse, and a number of lithographs by Matisse and Picasso. Once we visited the sisters shortly after a Manet portrait of a Madame somebody-or-other, done in pastels, had been delivered and was standing against the piano, ready to be framed. That day a new maid had come to work for the sisters. We had been invited for lunch, and while we were waiting for the ladies to dress, the maid was going around with a feather duster. Before I could stop her, she was dusting the pastels off the Manet painting, and the more she dusted, the more dust came floating from the portrait. I ran to her and stopped her.

"You're ruining the painting!" I exclaimed.

The maid was disconsolate. "What shall I do? I shall lose my job!"

"Wait." I had a little pastel box in my bag and I began retouching the portrait of Madame so-and-so. Then William added a few touches of silver gray coloring in the background, and we rubbed it all in with a handkerchief. We finished the portrait before the sisters came in for lunch.

The Cone sisters frequently invited us to their apartments, and they would regale us with stories about Gertrude Stein and her brother, Leo. They recounted how they first met Matisse in Paris when he was an obscure, struggling artist, at the insistence of Gertrude Stein. They were visiting their cousin in Paris, and she suddenly announced that she was going to introduce them to her friend, Matisse, who was having a hard time surviving financially as an artist. They were taken to Matisse's apartment, which was, as the French say, *sous les toits de Paris,* under the roofs of Paris. The Cone sisters brought along a basket of fruit as a gift. Matisse placed the fruit on the small terrace in the sunlight. In this one-room studio, a painting, apparently of Mrs. Matisse, was perched on an easel. The sisters looked at each other in horror. The painting was awful in their opinion. Madame Matisse was doing some millinery work to help pay the rent, and for her sitting she had put on a large yellow straw hat, topped by a long, black ostrich feather, which looked like it had been dipped in water. Its strands had become entangled in her black hair, which hadn't been combed. She seemed cross-eyed. When the sisters returned to the hotel, Eta said to Clarabel, "How could Matisse do this to such a pretty woman as his wife?"

However, the painting began to haunt the sisters. They were strangely bewitched by it.

The next morning they decided to have another look at it. They went by horse and carriage to the Matisse apartment and climbed the five flights of stairs. When they reached the top, Madame Matisse met them.

"You'll have to wait, Demoiselles, there's someone in the studio with my husband."

Finally they were ushered in, but the painting was nowhere in sight. The basket of fruit was still out on the terrace.

Eta said, "Your fruit is still there in the sun. Don't you want to take it in and eat it?"

Madame Matisse shrugged her shoulders. "That fruit is not for eating; it's for painting."

When asked about the portrait of his wife, Matisse reluctantly took out the painting and showed it to them. They looked at it for several minutes.

"How much did you say it was?"

He told them the price.

"But that isn't the price you quoted us yesterday."

"Well, I will confess, mademoiselles, that there was a gentleman here and he made me an offer for this painting. If you wish to have it, that's the best I can do."

The sisters conferred. "Why should someone else get the painting? We'll take it!"

They arranged to have the painting delivered, and as they were returning to their hotel, Clarabel remarked, "It really is a shocking painting."

At dinnertime, the sisters' brother, Sidney, who was studying medicine at the Sorbonne, visited them. "I have something very interesting to report to you."

"We have something exciting to tell *you*," Eta replied, and proceeded to tell him about the painting of the woman with the yellow hat and the black plume.

"My God, you didn't buy it!" Sidney interrupted.

"Yes we did."

It turned out that he was the one who had made Matisse the offer for the work.

The French artists have a system. If a French artist allows someone to purchase a picture he considers to be a major one, the customer must promise to buy an additional painting every year. Matisse made such an arrangement with the Cone sisters, and they bought his work steadily for the next thirty years. Picasso made the same arrangement with the sisters. A number of the early paintings of Picasso were inspired by the Cone sisters, who used to walk around Paris cutting a striking figure in their tightly laced bodices and long dresses covered with ruffles. They were portly women with heavy-lidded eyes, jet black hair, and strong features. Over the years, we maintained a friendship with the sisters. They often said that they would have made the same arrangement with us as they had with Picasso and Matisse if they had been younger. However, they did remain interested in our work, and continued to buy several of our works for their collection.

When Matisse came to visit in 1930, the sisters took him to the Baltimore Museum of Art to see our dual exhibit. Matisse told Eta that he found the quality of our work to be healthy and expressive and that it had the feeling of the growing element of this new country.

8
Our Friends, Students, and Collectors

One of the most absorbing aspects of William's career was his experiences in teaching aspiring artists, some of whom went on to become highly successful. The satisfaction of transmitting one's knowledge to others and the pleasure of seeing them come into their own can be appreciated only by those who have accepted the challenge of teaching.

One of our earliest pupils was Louise Nevelson, who became a celebrated sculptress. She had shown great talent at a very early age. She came to us through a recommendation by David Sarnoff. I could sense that she was potentially more talented as a sculptress than as a painter, for she had an unusual feeling for form. She was always piling things up on canvas, striving to get structure into her ideas. She was a beautiful young woman with classic features combined with a most lively expression. Later, when the Whitney showed her work, she acknowledged that we were her early teachers.

The first pupil we ever had was Mary Pomeroy Robinson. She was tall and comely with a remarkably placid disposition and a great love for art. I met Mary when I was in Gloucester before I was engaged to William. She studied with me. We would go out to Bass Rocks and sit on the high part of the rocks and paint the coast. I explained to her the nature of these rocks, that they were really the stern and barren coast, and how they had guarded the continent until the time the Pilgrims came here. I tried to give her the feeling of their permanence.

One of our friends was Dr. A. L. Goldwater, who summered in Gloucester. He had been my doctor. His wife said to us at one time, "You know, A. L. is getting deaf. If you could teach him a little painting it would be a great comfort. It would give him something to do and to think about."

One morning we took Dr. Goldwater with our class to paint on the docks as the fishermen sat around mending their nets.

William told the doctor, "I'm going to pick a daisy and you're going to paint it."

"I don't know how."

"Don't worry," William assured him. "The daisy has a yellow center, like the sun, and the white petals are like the rays of the sun. Make a round circle and put rays around it and we'll paint the yellow and the white." They did this. Then William handed him a glass cup, and said, "Put the glass in the picture, just the way you see it." After a while, Dr. Goldwater had a little painting of a glass with a daisy in it. He was very proud of his picture. William gave him a frame and he took it back to his hotel. All of the doctor's friends admired the painting.

"Why, you're a born primitive artist!" they told him.

A primitive he remained because he kept painting in the same manner. William never corrected his technique. He continued to tell him, "Paint what you see." Dr. Goldwater painted a dory on the water, and William showed him how to make little red brick houses. The doctor became adept. After the third lesson, he arrived at the studio with a big black ascot tie and a smock, and he wore a beret. We went down to the wharf and one of the fishermen came over to William and said, "He's your teacher, isn't he?" William said, "Yes."

William strove to instill a sense of purpose in his pupils. Lee, one of our students, tried to sell the first etching he made. When William heard about it, he asked Lee why he wanted to sell it.

"It was your first venture, you should want to keep it."

"My mother told me that if I want to wear silk shirts, I'd have to sell my work."

William shook his head. "I don't think that silk shirts are the most important part of being an artist. You're a splendid looking boy. You'd look fine in any kind of clothing, but if you want to wear the most expensive clothes, you should be in a profession that will net you a high income. Art may not be your best choice."

As it turned out, Lee became an illustrator working in a much more lucrative field.

Bena and Ralph Mayer were students too. He was the chemist who wrote *The Artists' Handbook*.

We sometimes had difficulty with pupils who started out painting, discovered that they were good, and concluded that they were ready to become professionals overnight. One beautiful young woman decided she was going to separate from her husband and launch a career as an interior decorator on her own. She gave a party to which she invited all her friends and announced her intentions. But nothing happened; she didn't receive any jobs. She got in touch with her husband, telling him she was ready to return to him. But he refused to take her back.

The talented young artist Mona Aarons was one of our pupils in Gloucester. She posed for William with her daughter Resa, and they were the inspiration for many of William's mother and child motifs that he was so fond of painting.

A number of our pupils were doctors and psychiatrists, and they invariably made good students. They were responsive and had the ability to concentrate. There was, for instance, Dr. Fenton, who went with us to Duck Pond where he made his first etching. He drew William sitting on a rock, and then drew me painting on another rock. He put in a tree and the pond. William came over and, seeing the drawing, said, "You have Adam and Eve in the Garden of Eden." Dr. Fenton laughed heartily. William retaliated by making a portrait of Dr. Fenton sitting in the garden etching. An unusual feature of the painting was that there was no chair, although Dr. Fenton was in a seated position. William called it *The Doctor/Psychiatrist*.

Mrs. Swan Hennessy, with her son, Patrice, came to America in 1929 on a voyage of sentiment to visit her deceased husband's birthplace in Rockford, Illinois. They lived in Paris and were traveling by boat when they met some friends of ours. Our friends suggested that Mrs. Hennessy and her son should spend the summer in Gloucester and then proceed to Illinois. They gave Mrs. Hennessy our name and address. However, when she got there, she had lost the information and only knew that we were artists who lived in Gloucester.

The Hennessys stayed at Merrill Hall, a small hotel on Eastern Point Road. Determined to find us, Mrs. Hennessy searched all the artists' studios. One afternoon she heard someone say, "I guess we can go over to the Meyerowitz's this evening. They're having open house." Mrs. Hennessy said, "Are these people artists?" "Of course." "Then could we join you?" And they brought Mrs. Hennessy and Patrice.

When we showed her some of our work, Mrs. Hennessy said, "I remember seeing your paintings at the Gallery Ingres in Paris. I recognize the style of the pictures."

She asked me to paint a portrait of her son for his twenty-first birthday, which was July 18. Throughout the following days, Patrice spent most of his time at our studio. He was intrigued by the atmosphere and activities surrounding him. He heard we were planning a visit to the Hales in Folly Cove and said he would take us there. We said we always went by bus, early in the morning. He said he would get an auto.

The next day Patrice was in a car, waiting to take us out. We drove to the Hales, and everyone was delighted with the visit.

On our way back home, Patrice was sweeping around the roads with much éclat to show us how well he could drive. He was going fast, and I said, "Generally a policeman jumps out of the bushes at this curve." At that moment, out jumped a policeman! "Stop! You won the race." Patrice turned to us. "What race did I win?" The policeman said, "You were going so fast you passed another car. Show me your license."

Patrice looked in his pocket and said, "Well I don't happen to have a license. I just got the car."

The policeman asked, "What's your name?"

"My name is Patrice Hennessy."

"Don't play jokes on me. You're Patrick." He wrote down the name. "Well you can tell your whole story to the judge next Monday morning." He handed Patrice a summons.

When we got home, I made dinner in the pressure cooker. Patrice was disturbed. He sat down, and suddenly the valve started steaming. He jumped up just in time. A great squirt flew from the pressure cooker. The stew was all over the ceiling. Patrice's suit was ruined. "What an awful day I've had!"

I said, "Let's clean up the kitchen, and maybe we'll think of something to save you." Then it occurred to me that the policemen held a ball about that time of year. Maybe, if we got tickets for the ball, that would placate the judge. I suggested that Patrice tell the judge about the journey to his father's birthplace, and that while on the way, he and his mother chose to visit Gloucester. Now, he would take all our pupils to the policemen's ball. Patrice was saved.

Patrice always carried a $50 bill in his pocket, and when we would take him out for tea or ice cream, no one could make change for it so we always paid for him. Finally, the pupils and I devised a plan so that the right change would be available.

For the policemen's fancy dress ball, we dressed up ten of our pupils, and we waited for Patrice. When he arrived we asked if he had the money for the tickets. Of course, he had the same $50 bill. But this time, the policemen at the ball had the right change! The loss of the grand $50 put quite a dent in Patrice's self-image.

As the summer waned, Mrs. Hennessy made plans for her trip to Rockford, Illinois. She had posed for William, and he made a beautiful etching of her; I had completed my portrait of Patrice. The name of the place they were going to somehow rang a bell in my mind. William and I then remembered that we knew a Mr. Boehland who owned a department store. He had been the first person to buy one of William's etchings in color, *The Fishermen at Sunrise,* done in Folly Cove. I wrote to Mr. Boehland and gave Mrs. Hennessy a letter of introduction. She got a wonderful reception from him. It turned out that Mr. Boehland was a school chum of her late husband, Swan Hennessy.

Swan Hennessy had left home at an early age to seek his fortune. He was a brilliant young man, and he became the partner of Edward McCormick of the National Harvester Company in Chicago. Hennessy told McCormick, "When I make my first million, I'm going to retire." That's what he did. He went to Paris and became the founder of the Three Star Hennessy Company, a very successful distillery concern. He had always loved music, and in Paris he devoted himself to composing. Mrs. Hennessy gave William the songs her husband had composed, and William sang them.

Professor Selman Waksman invited us to his home. He discovered streptomycin while at Rutgers University. He arranged the exhibition of our works with the Friends of Art of New Brunswick in 1947.

Moshe and Fania Penn were devoted to us and equally indulgent toward young people by encouraging them to develop their talents. The Penns fostered writers, musicians, and artists. Moshe was a doctor, and Fania looked like a gypsy. She was always preparing *latkes* (pancakes) to serve at a Jewish meal. They were hospitable and enjoyed introducing their friends to one another. The Penns lived in the heart of Williamsburg. We used to go over the Brooklyn Bridge at twilight in order to be there in time for dinner. William painted the doctor, and I painted Fania.

An early chum of William's was Lawrence Miller, whom he briefed in architecture. Lawrence was an optometrist who took care of our eyes and prescribed glasses. We in turn gave him our paintings and etchings. He had two beautiful daughters, Estelle and Maxine. Mrs. Miller had a beautiful voice, and she and William sang duets together.

Mr. and Mrs. Lang Goldsmith had left their extensive factories in Germany. They had three daughters, Marian, Eleanor, and Doris. Marian studied with us, but she died in her teens. The Goldsmiths then requested that we do a portrait of her. I gave William some drawings, and he combined his impression and made a beautiful portrait capturing her personality. Thereafter, we remained staunch friends, and Mrs. Goldsmith was a fine musician as well as a hostess on our various Boston exhibitions at Doll and Richards Gallery.

William was requested to give a lecture in Yiddish at the home of Felix Warburg, an event that marked the beginning of the Jewish Museum. In the forties the various institutions, including the *Jewish Daily Forward,* were desirous of promoting the Yiddish language. They asked several artists, including Jacques Lipshitz and William Zorach, neither of whom could go beyond a few phrases in Yiddish. William regaled us with a vivid description of the flexibility of the language in adapting to the native land of the Jewish masses, be it Russia, Germany, or America. His opening phrase was, "Bie uns ist herein gemovt a neuya familia," meaning, "Next door to us a new family moved in." Then he mixed Russian and Yiddish, then French and Yiddish, and the effect was hilarious. Over three hundred people attended the lecture. He spoke in Yiddish about Shalom Aleichem and said that one of the remarkable things about his stories was that whatever happened, Shalom Aleichem always spoke in the first person, as though it was happening to him, and this idiomatic style has been used by writers like Aleksandr Solzhenitsyn. It made the stories very personal and gave them a poignant quality. William's lecture told about the revival of the Yiddish language.

PESACH

Pesach, or Passover, is the yearly festival that celebrates the advent of freedom, when Moses led the children of Israel out of Egypt, releasing them from their bondage. This is commemorated with great joy and feasting. It is significant for the cohesion of families.

For over thirty years we were invited to join Rabbi David De Sola Pool and his family—his wife Tamar and their daughter Naomi and son Ithiel—for Pesach. The first time we were invited to their home adjacent to the synagogue. The event became so popular that later it was held in a large hall in the temple. This is the oldest Spanish and Portuguese Synagogue in America. Our first Pesach with them was in 1925. They only knew that we were artists. Naomi, who was then a young child, asked William if he could read her a passage in Hebrew. After hearing William read, they always wanted to have him return. Every Pesach, William and the rabbi would officiate. The rabbi would do the speaking, and William would do the singing. There was a room in the temple where the *kiddush*, or blessing, was given after the service. The room had a skylight that could be opened when they wanted to perform a marriage ceremony. The room's capacity was a hundred people. Very often they held the *Pesach* with a full house.

Among the guests were the Rothschilds, judges from the Supreme Court of the State of New York, the writer Fannie Hurst, and the sculptor Jacques Lipshitz. Ms. Hurst, who was present throughout the years, always wanted to sit next to William to hear him speak in Hebrew, with an English translation. Tamar introduced us to Eliazer Ben-Yehuda and his wife. He was the philologist who had transformed Hebrew into a living tongue, which was to become the cohesive expression of the people of Israel. He wrote the dictionary that became the source of Modern Hebrew. We were thrilled to meet them.

Another person who posed for William and inspires warm memories was little Winnie Graham, the daughter of one of our collectors. One day we took Winnie to the zoo. When she saw the animals, she asked, "Can they talk to each other?"

"Why, of course!" William replied.

"Uncle Billy, what do they say?"

"They go to parties together and they play music and they listen to each other singing."

"Oh! I'd love to go to one of their parties!"

William took her back to our studio and, while he drew the different animals for her, I told her a story.

"The lion is an important animal. He's the head of them all. He's conducting an orchestra. The zebras are dancing in striped suits. The monkeys are playing little accordions. They're making a lot of noise, but everybody's enjoying it. The giraffe was above them with his head in the air. The birds do a little singing—like sopranos. Some of the wolves howl a bit. There is a lot of music going on in the animal world."

Winnie was fascinated, she burst out, "I'd love going to an animal concert!"

William put her in the center of a painting with all the animals grouped around her, playing their various instruments. He called it *Winnie in the Zoo*.

Our friends and collectors brought us a rich mixture of experiences. One good friend, Erich Cohn, was the head of the Goodman Matzoh Company. He became interested in William's work. The Cohns owned a collection of modern German art, including several Corinths, Noldes, and Beckmans. He loaned his collection, including William's work, to the Museum of Modern Art.

Our pupil Helen Stein introduced her friend Bobbie Miller to us. Bobbie was a woman wrestler who kept a .22 caliber rifle in her car. She wanted to convert to Judaism so William taught her how to make horseradish.

Two other dear friends were Rose and Hyman Harmon. They were interior decorators who restored the furnishings for the Flagler Museum in Palm Beach, Florida. We were invited to spend Sabbath evenings at their home, where William would officiate. William would usher in the meal with a *kiddush,* using the old wine cup that Rose's father had brought from Russia. The little silver wine cups for the Sabbath services were frequently the only family heirlooms that immigrants brought with them to America, hiding them inside their clothes. Sometimes immigrants would bring a samovar to the United States, as William's mother Shendl did.

His grandfather's samovar was large, and it took two men to carry and place it on the table. It had carved wooden handles and had to be stoked like a furnace. William kept his mother's samovar in his studio. He would throw in a few pieces of paper and old canvas stretchers that he had chopped up for firewood. When the pot was boiling hot, the water would start to bubble. Tea never tasted so good as it did from Shendl's samovar. Immigrants sometimes brought *betgewant*—great big goosefeather pillows and quilts or bedding. These would have money sewn into them, and would be given to the bride by her parents and friends in the village. It was the customary dowry.

Rose Harmon once presented us with a large black cabinet from China. The interior was red lacquer into which William placed *The Discussion,* the etching in color. When Rabbi Zev Nelson visited us from Boston, the first thing he noticed was this etching. He exclaimed, "I've got to have it." Rabbi Nelson not only bought the etching, but the cabinet as well, so that he could keep the total emotional impact he had received when he walked into our studio.

Thirty original first edition etchings of *The Discussion* were acquired by collectors, among whom was the president of Israel, Zalman Shazar. This was the largest edition William ever made of any particular etching.

The enthusiasm engendered by this etching was remarkable. Valerie Walter bought a print and took it home with her to Baltimore. She placed it in an alcove in her living room and it became the cynosure for all her guests. One afternoon when she came home, the etching had disappeared. She never found out how. In desperation she wrote to William, "I must get another *Discussion*. It has vanished from my home. This time I will not put it in the alcove. I'll attach it to the wall enclosed in a heavy frame." William made another print for her.

Mr. and Mrs. Joel Glass were enthusiastic collectors. Their daughter Sarah Ellen was about eleven years old when we dressed her in an early American bodice of green velvet with lace and ruffles for both William and me to paint. Joel Glass, an editor of the *Boston Globe,* interviewed us for his newspaper. William painted him as the Joel mentioned in the Bible, with a basket of fruit. I painted him as a busy newspaper editor with a pipe clenched between his teeth.

Among the people attracted to William's work was A. C. Goodyear, a former president of the Museum of Modern Art. Mrs. Hattie Speed gave William an exhibition at the Speed Museum in Louisville, which also was the home of Justice Brandeis. William had already made one of his most noteworthy etchings of the justice.

We met the Carpenters in a curious way. One day while we were at home in New York, William received a telephone call from a man who asked, "Have you got the still life with an open window, a little cottage in the distance, a Ford outside and, close by, a tray with plums and a window curtain blowing? Bring me this painting before midnight and I will buy it."

William surmised that the caller had seen this painting at an exhibition. "If you want it, come over and get it," he said.

"I can't come over. I don't have time to look at it because I want it by midnight. If you want to sell the painting, bring it to me. I'm in Germantown, Pennsylvania."

I took the phone and said, "If you really mean it, I'll bring the painting to you. How do I get there?"

"Take a train. I'll be waiting for you at the 30th Street Station in Philadelphia. My name is Carpenter."

"Are you really going?" William queried. "We're expecting guests, you know."

"I've already prepared the sandwiches, and I think I should go." I packed the painting in corrugated board and took the train to Philadelphia.

When I stepped off at the 30th Street Station, a man approached.

"I trust you're Mrs. Meyerowitz? My wife is waiting at the newsstand."

Mrs. Carpenter and I held the painting carefully between us in the car to keep the frame from being bumped up and down. It was twilight when we arrived at a country house with a lovely garden. Mrs. Carpenter prepared drinks and her husband unpacked the painting. "You know, I've never seen this, but my wife wanted it badly." He looked at it for a while. "I like it, too. The painting no longer belongs to Mr. Meyerowitz. It is ours. Let's call up your husband and tell him the happy news."

Mrs. Carpenter explained. It seems that the couple were discussing their approaching wedding anniversary. Mr. Carpenter said he wanted to buy an antique diamond ring.

"I'd much prefer to have a Meyerowitz," Mrs. Carpenter rejoined.

"What is that?"

She told him it was a painting she had seen of William's at the Art Alliance, where an exhibition called "Collectors' Choice" had been, and she had fallen in love with this work.

Mr. Carpenter decided to look up William. He went to the public library, consulted *Who's Who*, found our address, and got the telephone number from the operator.

The Carpenters invited me to stay overnight but I told them I wanted to go to a hotel in Philadelphia to visit my pupil, Ms. Lippincott. They said, "We'll take you. Where is it?" I said it's at 11th Street and Locust and it's called the Clinton.

They exclaimed, "Oh, that's the hotel where we spent our wedding night!"

Mina and Ralph Tropp, a couple who had owned restaurants in New York, were also our friends as well as close friends of Golda Meir. When they retired, they moved to Tryon, North Carolina. Mina is an artist of pressed flowers. We spent many happy occasions with them. William did a portrait of Ralph, and I painted one of Mina.

The members of William's family include Rosalyn Tureck, the pianist, who is a Bach exponent. She used to invite us to her rehearsals, attended only by her sister Margaret, her manager. She asked William to paint her portrait.

William's niece Barbara De Angeles composes musicals. Laura Nyro, another niece, is the composer and singer whose albums have been issued by Columbia Records.

A very early friend of William's was Jacob Moscowitz, who was an architect. William introduced him to Henrietta, an accountant, and they became husband and wife. The Harmons introduced us to Mr. and Mrs. Friedless, who became collectors of our work. Leo Rovinger, an early friend of William's, was a musical composer from the Federal Settlement house. He married Beatrice, who ran a catering business.

A Russian tenor, Maxim Karolik, often sang duets with William in our New York studio and Gloucester. The Karolik work is in the Boston Fine Arts Museum.

Young people who were an inspiration to both of us were Tatiana Tremaine and later Diane Dawson, who became a valued assistant.

9

Justices of the Supreme Court

In 1921 William was having a show at the Corcoran Gallery in Washington. A tall, distinguished gentleman in his seventies wandered around looking at William's etchings, which were in cases covered by heavy plate glass at the entrance to the upper gallery in the vestibule.

"I have actually come here to look at a portrait of Chief Justice White," explained this man. "But I am intrigued by your etchings and I want to buy some. Young man, you have quite an establishment here."

William said, "I'm glad you like the etchings. But I feel I'm only beginning."

"I feel the same way," countered the stranger. "I expect to retire in a year or so and devote the rest of my life to writing."

William asked, "What do you do?"

"I am a justice of a Court. Let me select the etchings I want to acquire."

He slid the glass slabs and picked the works he desired. They were a set of Gloucester etchings—*Early Morning* and *Bright Summer Day*, among others. He almost bumped into the plate glass slabs. I held him back.

"You have saved my life, young lady," he muttered. "I could have broken my glasses and perhaps injured my eyesight."

"I have helped the handsomest men to visit our exhibition," I replied.

After exchanging further pleasantries he remarked, "I'd like to give you the money."

"But we cannot accept it. You have to go down to the office of the director, Mr. Minnegerode."

"Well, let's go." The man gathered up the etchings and strode down the marble stairs and we followed. Reaching the office, he said, "I want to buy these etchings, but the young artist says he has to wait a month or two to get the money. I know artists need money to survive, and I want you to give him the cash right away."

Mr. Minnegerode replied that he would.

William said, "You're very unusual. Most people don't care whether artists need money or not."

As the customer paid William, he said, "Show your wife Washington. Take her to a show this evening; give her a good time."

When he left, William turned to Mr. Minnegerode. "Who was that gentleman?"

"Why, don't you know? He is Justice Oliver Wendell Holmes of the Supreme Court."

At the Hotel Bellevue a day or so later I received a letter from Mrs. Holmes. "Please influence your husband to etch a portrait of the Justice." William replied he would like to etch the justice at the Supreme Court. The judge sent us a note. "It is not permissible to draw or photograph while the Court is in session. However, I'll pose for you at my home on I Street."

Justice Holmes then took a lively interest in William's work. He invited us to visit him at his home in Beverly Farms, Massachusetts. It was a summer morning when we arrived. Mrs. Holmes was in the garden gathering flowers for her table.

"I'm sorry," she announced. "The justice will not be able to be with us today because he's busy with the Sacco and Vanzetti case." He was in favor of delaying their executions.

We visited with the judge's wife for several hours, finding her charming company. Mrs. Holmes, who was a diminutive woman, never walked alongside the justice, but always followed him. It was a quaint sight to behold—the six-foot judge with his tiny wife trailing behind him. Mrs. Holmes was a Quaker and a passionate pacifist.

Noting a tree that towered over the house, we remembered the story that we had heard. As a youth, Holmes had tried his hand at etching. The subject he had chosen was this tree. Following instructions in an art book, he dipped his plate in acid. Consulting his watch, he counted the minutes that the plate was to be immersed. His father—the noted author, Dr. Oliver Wendell Holmes, Sr.—passed by and knocked on the door of his room.

"There's a strong odor of acid permeating the atmosphere. What are you doing?"

"I'm trying to make an etching," his son replied.

"Well, my boy, you'd better be a barrister."

Once, when we called on Holmes, the justice strode out of the door to greet us. "I've been reading books on modern art so I can chat more intelligently on the subject."

"That isn't necessary," William said. "We want to talk about *your* experiences."

"Well," replied Holmes, "my greatest experience was undoubtedly the time I enlisted as a soldier in the Civil War. I was sixteen, and I was sent immediately to the front. The first thing that happened was that a bullet struck me in the upper left clavicle." He pointed to it. "The bullet is still there. Although I was very sick, the doctors decided that they would not risk removing it, so I still have it with me."

Ellen Day Hale was living in Washington and she invited us to a Thursday afternoon tea in the home of Justice and Mrs. Brandeis. The house was furnished with early American mahogany furniture. There was a samovar, but it had a leak. William took some rubber bands, fastened a washer on the cock spout, and got the samovar back into working order.

Justice Brandeis was a tall, lanky man, and when he wrapped himself in his gray flannel shawl, he bore a startling resemblance to Abraham Lincoln. He and Justice Holmes were close friends. Shortly after William finished a portrait etching of Holmes, Mrs. Brandeis said to me, "I would like William to etch a portrait of my husband." William did so the following summer in Hyannis, where the Brandeises had their summer home. The Brandeises' residence was on a hill with a windmill. The scene was so picturesque that William sketched the house and the windmill before we rang the doorbell to announce our arrival.

Justice Brandeis was alone. He told us, "I sent the family off on a picnic so that you would have complete privacy for your work."

In Justice Brandeis's study, a number of books were heaped in one corner. "This is my life's work," he explained. "Everything I have thought and worked for I have incorporated in this little group of books."

When Brandeis University, named for the justice, was founded, we were invited to be present at the opening ceremonies, and several of William's portraits of Louis Brandeis were on display. We sat with the Brandeis family, including their daughter, Mrs. Gilbert, who was a lawyer, like her father.

William ended up doing portraits not only of Holmes and Brandeis but also of most of their colleagues on the Supreme Court. Their personalities varied widely. Justice Harlan Stone, for instance, had a genial, outgoing personality, and he was very much interested in art.

"The other justices on the bench are not very knowledgeable about art, but Holmes and I were imbued with it from our earliest years," Justice Stone told us.

William drew Justice Stone in his library. William started at seven in the morning and worked until eleven, at which time the justice was scheduled to be at Court. Stone put us in his car and took us over there so we could study him and his colleagues while they worked.

We sketched Justice Stone while he was at work on reviewing briefs. Every now and then he would assume a pose for us, and we would sketch furiously. I painted him and William etched him.

During one such sitting, Justice Stone announced, "I expect to be interviewed today, if you don't mind. Don't pay any attention to what we're saying. Just keep working." In the midst of the interview, the Justice turned to us. "I want to show Max Lerner (the interviewer) my art collection. Won't you come with us?" He opened the door leading to an adjoining room, a combination library and living room, and he showed the reporter his etchings of celebrated English justices and his valued portraits of Holmes and Cardozo. When he came to the Cardozo picture, his eyes filled with tears, for Cardozo had recently passed away. William had etched Cardozo at the request of Dean Landis of the Harvard Law School. It was one of his finest works.

Justice Benjamin Cardozo, whose portrait, done by William, had so touched Justice Stone, was a wonderful writer. Cardozo was a close friend of Governor Lehman of New York. He was a serious, melancholy looking man, and he was extremely fond of music. He invited me to a concert at Convention Hall in Washington and proved a most gracious escort.

William was also asked to do portraits of Justices Murphy and Black as well. The latter had exquisite hands. William also did portraits of Justice Douglas and of Justice Felix Frankfurter. Frankfurter was born in Vienna. Because of his brilliance he was appointed to the highest legal tribunal of the United States. Like Holmes, Frankfurter had come from the Harvard Law School, which acquired a number of William's etchings.

William's portraits of the Supreme Court justices have been bought by a number of universities. Harvard, as noted, bought a series for the Langdell Hall Law School; George Washington University acquired some, as did Yale, the University of Pennsylvania, and the University of Michigan. Brandeis has some of the portraits, and some are in private collections.

Justice Owen J. Roberts was a tall, stately man. We studied him in his chambers at the Supreme Court. He was gracious about not accepting any visitors while we were with him. He would go out into the anteroom to receive his guests. He had a farm in

Bill in 1944

Pennsylvania, and among the etchings that he acquired was *The Farm*—an etching in color. Subsequently, President Franklin Roosevelt asked him to investigate the Pearl Harbor incident.

The portraits done by William of the Supreme Court justices were a historic event.

We were asked by a young lawyer, Samuel Lepler, to paint a portrait of Jacob Javits. We were taken down to City Hall and ushered in to the Attorney General's office, where Javits was dictating to a secretary. He greeted us cordially, and we set up our easels near the large window. William said, "Go right on with your work and we'll do ours," with no further conversation to interfere with the affairs of the City of New York. The second sitting took place in the Javits apartment on Park Avenue, where Mrs. Javits, a charming woman, greeted us. There was a large armchair near a refectory table, and we continued to study the mobile features which revealed a brilliant mentality. The third sitting took place in our studio, where the conversation became lively, and William was able to produce a fine likeness on canvas. When the portrait was completed, there was an unveiling at the "21 Club" before a large assembly of legal confrères. At our table sat Jack Dempsey and his wife and Mr. Javits's brother, also a distinguished lawyer. The portrait was presented to the Republican Club.

It was in Washington that we met President Herbert Hoover. He visited the exhibition in the Corcoran Gallery and left his card. We were introduced to him and he complimented William on his "art on metal" because of his own experience as a mining engineer.

10

Mexico

IN 1956 WE VISITED MEXICO WHERE THE SPECTACULAR SCENERY AND THE PEOPLE WE ENcountered made a deep impression on us.

In Mexico City we met the writer Michael Glantz who owned a café near our hotel which was a meetingplace of the international set of writers and artists. The café was open to the street, and one pushed through a beaded curtain to enter. The waitresses were señoritas who wore long, flowing skirts and white peasant blouses with puffed sleeves. They asked us in Spanish if we would like some borscht and gefilte fish.

We went to the museums and saw the great murals by Mexico's famous artists—Diego Rivera and Orozco, whom we knew personally. Orozco produced his tremendous wall decorations with his only arm. At the cathedral we sketched people praying on their knees. Then we walked on the streets and drew little girls in their native clothes. At the town hall we saw murals by Rivera. The people in the murals seemed to follow us out into the square.

From Mexico City we boarded a bus for Taxco, the celebrated artists' colony. The bus had to climb mountains and traverse valleys bristling with cactus. Beside the road we saw horsemen and people working on the tremendous ranches.

When we got off the bus at Taxco, night was already falling. We were expecting to go to the Hotel Victoria. But it was impossible to find it in the dark. Instead of walking further, we approached a lit doorway and asked for a "Comoda." This turned out to be the Hotel Santa Prisca, whose proprietor had been a student at the Pennsylvania Academy of Art. He was happy to welcome us. He made us comfortable in a corner room where we could look down on the fountain spraying in the town square, and see the peasants coming and going about their work.

Our stay in Taxco was delightful. One night we walked up a hill in the moonlight and entered a shop. I was searching for a particular kind of silver ring with a topaz. It was for a young friend of mine who had lost such a ring. And, sure enough, in a glass case, I saw one. I said to the young man operating the shop, "Please reserve that ring. I'll return tomorrow to pay for it."

The next morning we climbed the hill, but to our amazement the shop wasn't there. It was as if the ground had swallowed it up. We walked back and forth around the area, but there wasn't a trace of it.

As we walked down to the other side of the hill, we came upon another little shop displaying handmade silver crafts. I told the proprietor, "There was another store in this vicinity last night, but it's disappeared."

"I know. That often happens here," he said.

"What do you mean?" I asked.

He explained, "A shopkeeper will open a couple of nights for business and then close and merge with a bigger shop down in the main square. I don't know which outfit your shop has merged into."

"Why do they take all that trouble to set up business on the hill?" I asked.

"Because on certain days they expect some tourists to climb the hill. They stay for them and then disappear."

Then we designed the ring, and Sigi, the young shopkeeper, made it for us.

We traveled on to Cuernavaca, where the climate is the same the year round. We stayed at a hotel high up on a mountain. Down below was a rose garden and a swimming pool. We had dinner in a house across from the hotel that served as a dining hall. Next door was a place with a sign, "Salon De Acte," over the door. I asked somebody, "What does that mean?"

"It means drama studio."

However, when we entered the chamber, we were astounded to discover that it was a synagogue. Mexico is a Catholic country, and other religions have a low profile. The Jews were not allowed to call their place of worship a synagogue, but an "actors' studio." William attended a service. Some of the celebrants, noticing a stranger in their midst, asked him to recite a few prayers, which he did so well that the president of the synagogue invited us to have tea with his family that afternoon.

"We live right next door," he explained. "You walk along the wall and come to a big gate. When you pull the bell, I will be out in my garden waiting for you."

When we walked through the gate, we found ourselves in a tropical jungle of coffee plants, palms, and Mexican fruit trees. In the center was a little gazebo in which we sat and were served tea on a table of cedar wood. William asked our host, Dr. Kon, "How is it that you settled in Mexico?"

"I came here to escape the Nazis," our host explained. "I owned a textile factory in Warsaw. My goods were sold all over Europe. Then the Nazis arrived in Poland. I had seven children. The Nazis killed one of my sons. Luckily I was able to escape with the rest of my family. We decided to go to Mexico. Here I built a rooming house for travelers."

When he finished speaking, our host sang a prayer with a very old Jewish melody that he had known from his childhood in Poland. He stopped in the middle and turned to William.

"I bet you can't remember that melody."

William had taken a piece of paper from his sketch book, and he was writing down the notes as Dr. Kon sang them. Then he picked up his zither and sang the melody.

"You're the only one who has ever been able to remember this song and sing it back to me."

Dr. Kon was one of the "Brothers Ashkenazi" from the novel by I. J. Singer.

Proceeding from Taxco on our way to Acapulco, we took a bus to Pueblo, a very unusual old city. To get there we had to cross a series of mountain ranges. We traveled through scenic landscapes that must have suggested to the local people the patterns for the *rebozos*—the rugs and shawls that they wove, as well as the patterns of their *zapatos*, their shoes. After a delightful stay at Acapulco, on the West coast, we got on a bus for the return trip to the East coast.

Arriving in Mexico City, we met a collector of William's work, Mr. Youngster, who invited us to stay with him. He gave us the key to his home, which was on the outskirts of the city. The house was built from the lava of a volcano. It was a spackled black stone. One side of his house was completely made of glass. When the family wanted to enjoy the view, they pushed the glass aside and it was as if they were living in a tent. Just beyond them was an impoverished Mexican family who lived in a little hut. The oldest child, about three, took care of the baby who was a year old. Incidentally, I never heard a child cry while I was in Mexico, which I thought was quite unusual.

Mr. and Mrs. Youngster were hosts to many professional people, especially actors, who visited Mexico City. They owned a factory that made textiles. They took us to a vaudeville show where the women were nursing their babies and feeding dinner to the other children.

One of the skits on stage showed an American woman tourist wearing a bikini and black sunglasses, while an entourage of porters carried her clothes in an assortment of cases.

Wherever we went in Mexico we sketched in the outdoor markets, where all the merchandise was beautifully displayed. William sketched a lot of horses and scenery. Later, he developed these sketches for several panels of Mexican themes that he painted.

William Painting, 1948, photo by Al Puhn

11
Israel

WILLIAM'S ART, LIFE, AND CHARACTER WERE SHAPED BY, AND CONCERNED WITH, HIS Judaic origins, and we made thirteen trips to Israel. Our first trip was in 1952.

In Russia, William's father had been a member of the Lovers of Zion, a pioneer organization dedicated to the return to the Jewish homeland in Palestine. In America, he had joined the Friends of Zion, and when he died, William continued the membership. William made many paintings and etchings on the theme of *Herzl Showing the Land of Israel to the People*, with the words: "If you will it, it is not a dream."

At Madison Square Garden in New York in 1923, we were invited to attend the First Zionist Meeting in America. William made an etching of the event, and I made a painting of the convention, which is now hanging in the Jewish National Fund building, in New York. Professor Albert Einstein was guest of honor, and we were requested to make portraits of him.

We were seated on either side of him on the stage. The leading Zionists of the period were there—Weizmann, Ussishkin, Shmah Levin, Mosesohn, Maslansky, and Rubin Breinen. The Balfour Declaration was read by Weizmann. The speakers spoke of their dreams for the establishment of the new state, although it could not be said for certain that it would ever become a reality. Einstein's presence had an electrifying effect on everyone.

To study Einstein further, William was invited to attend a lecture on relativity given by the professor at New York University. They gave us seats in the front row where we could watch Einstein's every expression. William was particularly impressed by his deep-set eyes, enormous shock of hair, and large expressive hands.

There were two hundred professors listening. Einstein spoke in German, taking his theory from beginning to its logical conclusion. At the end he exclaimed, "Es ist ganz einfach," it is very simple. After that remark he left. Some professors rushed down and confronted us. "You took notes to the very end. Tell us what is your conclusion?" We gathered our sketches and rushed to the same exit. William made an etching of the professor in which only Einstein's head was visible, symbolized as a planet in space.

Einsteinian physics influenced William in his own application of light and shadow. William began incorporating into his work some of Einstein's theories regarding the speed of light as the refraction of the sun's rays bursting into a shower of light.

William also made a drawing, and I painted a portrait, of Henrietta Szold, the founder of Hadassah. Mrs. Szold, a Baltimorian, had arrived in Palestine in 1914 and realized that there was an acute need for medical help there. She organized a group that subsequently became worldwide in its scope and influence. She was instrumental in bringing thousands of refugee children, rescued from the Nazis, into Palestine where, under the auspices of Hadassah, they were educated and cared for until they could manage for themselves.

In subsequent years, William met and did portraits of many of the leaders of the new state of Israel.

In 1967 we attended a dinner of the Jewish Legion in Jerusalem where we were introduced to David Ben-Gurion. A man of medium height, with white hair, penetrating brown eyes, and a ringing voice, he told us that in the early years he served as a watchman at a kibbutz and helped put up barbed wire fence to protect the community against attack.

The Jewish Legion was holding its fiftieth anniversary, and William and I were invited to participate in the celebrations. Since the time of the ancient Maccabees, the Jewish Legion had been the first military unit of Jews who fought for their homeland. It served in Palestine during World War I under the British commander, Lord Allenby. William had friends who were members, among them Fred Mallot, the chairman, and William Braiterman, the historian of the legion. We met Golda Meir and Itzhak Rabin and toured Jerusalem with Teddy Kollek, the mayor.

Golda Meir told us how, when she first came to Israel, she worked in a kibbutz. There were only three tin cups for the entire community, and everything had to be shared.

We met the president of Israel, Zalman Shazar, who presented William with a book of his memoirs entitled *Morning Stars*. The book had been translated into English, and when William remarked that he would like to read it in its original Hebrew, President Shazar sent him the Hebrew version with the inscription, "You express yourself in color and I with words."

William contributed his works to many causes. At different times, he gave paintings and etchings to the United Jewish Appeal, the Hebrew University in Jerusalem, the Friends of Zion, and The Jewish National Fund.

The father of the modern Hebrew language was Eliazer Ben-Yehuda. His son, Ehud, came to the United States to lecture and to arrange for the publication of his father's dictionary in an English translation. We entertained Ehud during this visit, and he told us fascinating stories of the struggle his father had faced getting the modern Hebrew adopted by the state. Eliazer Ben-Yehuda had been thrown into jail by the Orthodox Jewish community on a trumped-up charge, after publishing the first newspaper in Hebrew—which was considered a sacrilege. His crime in the eyes of the traditionalists was that he had dared to modernize the sacred script. While he was in jail, his wife, Hemda, smuggled in pencils and pieces of paper so that he could add new words to the dictionary he was compiling.

Ehud invited us while we were in Israel to be guests of the Ben-Yehuda family.

We embarked on an oceanliner from the Cunard line bound for France. On the ship was a Yemenite rabbi who had features so striking that William was anxious to draw him. Whenever the Yemenite sat down to talk with his followers, William would sit nearby and surreptitiously make drawings. The rabbi got wind of this because his disciples would point to William.

He said, "You must not draw me because if you take away my features, I will not be able to meet the Almighty."

"I am not taking anything away," William answered. "I am making the world aware of your personality."

We stayed in Paris for several days. We had a lovely time, sketching the boulevards and the marketplaces. We sat by the Seine. In the Louvre, we practically wore our shoes off walking.

Then we drove to Orly Airport to catch our plane for Israel. We arrived during a fierce storm. We could hear the clang of metal as the mechanics strove to get our plane ready for the flight. It was a small, four-engine plane, and we were unable to take off until two in the morning. By that time, the storm had lifted but the wind was still blowing. As we entered the plane, I was holding William's hand so hard that I dug my nails into his hand. However, we made it; we emerged from the chrysalis of rough weather into the glory of sunny Israel.

For part of the visit, we stayed at the house of Dora Ben-Yehuda. We were given the study with its black cedarwood inlaid-with-pearl furniture given to Ben-Yehuda by an Arab philologist. There were hanging lamps above a shelf that contained a cast of Eliazer's right hand. The house was four miles from Jerusalem and was the second dwelling from the border of No-Man's Land. A spiral fence alongside the road had a sign reading "Beware of Bombs." The road commanded a brilliant view of Jerusalem nestling in the Judean hills like a jewel, gleaming with the Mount of Olives, the Wailing Wall, and the domes around the tomb of King David.

William and I painted the city of Jerusalem from the road where the bomb sign stood. Every morning before we started painting, we saluted the sentries posted by the Jordanian army across No-Man's Land by raising our canvases. They raised their weapons in reply. Behind us was a contingent of Israeli soldiers hidden by a grove of trees. In short, we worked between the two armies.

This was the first of many trips we were to make over the years. We painted and sketched every part of the little nation. Jerusalem continued to provide an inspired subject for us. We went into the marketplace to catch people going about their chores. There were little stands with awnings to shield them from the hot sun. Booths of Arab and Jewish vendors stood side by side or opposite each other. We used to stand behind a crate of vegetables and sketch the shoppers with their heavy plastic bags, the porters lugging merchandise on their shoulders, the housewives with their flowing aprons.

William painted the Wailing Wall from many angles. The first time he saw and sketched it was on our initial trip when we climbed to the roof of the Tomb of King David and looked down on the Wall. William sketched and painted the Mosque of Omar, which was constructed on the site of the second Temple of Solomon, and he did a large panel of Moses.

We visited Safed, the famous art colony of Israel, four hundred feet above sea level. William was asked by the mayor to carry the Torah in a religious procession. He did a painting of it which he called *Simcha Torah*, "the Joy of Torah." William carried a copper or zinc plate for etching wherever we went, as if it were a sketch pad.

On one occasion, while staying with the Talithmans outside Tel Aviv, we walked to the Yakon River, where the young people paddled canoes on weekends. We selected a picturesque bend of the river as the site for our work. It overlooked the industrial buildings of Tel Aviv in the distance. Within fifteen minutes we could reach the heart of the city, where we did a lot of sketching, sitting in a café on Dizingoff Street, which was named after the first mayor of the city. The street was lined with large green trees under which were rows of cafés with sidewalk tables. We would sketch the housewives who gathered at the cafés every morning after their husbands went to work and the children to school. Before they shopped, the women would convene in the cafés, greet each other, and read about the events of the day.

Over the years, as we visited Israel, we had the opportunity of seeing how spectacularly the country was expanding into a major center of culture.

Our visits to Israel afforded us the chance for reunions with cherished relatives and friends. A Jewish pioneer in Palestine had been Uncle Moshe, the brother of William's mother. One of his five children was Menachem Mittelman, William's first cousin, who became a specialist in agriculture. He was one of the first people to plant pecan trees in Israel with success. We met his wife, Tova, and their children. Ruth Halevi, a second cousin, was also descended from a sabra family. Her husband, Ariah, was head of the Wingate Institute, a sports complex in which army and navy personnel as well as Olympic athletes were trained.

In 1961 we traversed the Negev to Elath. There was just one road that we traveled on a bus. We returned by plane. In the Negev we visited King Solomon's Mines. In later trips we went across the Sinai to Sharm Al-Sheikh, to the Straits of Tiran, and to Mount Sinai where Moses had received the Ten Commandments.

The city of Yamit that Israel had built, and the settlements that flourished in the desert, were within our vision before they were returned to Egypt in the Camp David agreement between President Sadat and Prime Minister Begin.

Our numerous trips brought to life and wove into our artistic vision the age-old land of the Jews. They confirmed the meaning of William's heritage and reinforced his sense of purpose and the commitment of his conscience.

12

The Art of William Meyerowitz

WILLIAM SAID THAT ART WAS INVENTED BY MAN AS THE ANTIDOTE TO LIFE'S STRUGGLE. He believed that art was the embellishment of life.

When asked what "school" he belonged to, he said,

> What does it matter? I have been a diligent pupil of the National Academy of Design, and of the old masters. I have investigated old trends in all styles, and have become a student of nature and of life about me. Intuition and common sense have been my guide.
>
> I am independent, bound by the tenets of no narrow academic association, and prejudiced against no new discovery or movement. Form to me is the expression of objects and the evolution of nature.

He said that "Modern Art" is an erroneous term; it should be called "Contemporary Art." And, in fact, as soon as contemporary art is accepted, it takes its place in the world of timeless art. Every artist who is a classic today was the modern artist of yesterday.

A pupil once asked Meyerowitz, "How does one become an artist?"

He responded, "There are three rules. The first one is to draw, the second is to draw, and the third is to draw."

He observed, "What happens to a canvas is an unpredictable and surprising thing."

Julius Meier Graefe, the well-known art critic who discovered the lost paintings of Vermeer, and an authority on El Greco, came to our studio and expressed his revelation about William's work. He said, "Here is an artist whose healthy mind radiates against the dark clouds of psychotic expression."

Oscar Bluemner, the German architect and artist whose work was handled by Alfred Stieglitz, wrote about the strong sense of structure inherent in William's work. Irma Kraft, the drama critic, pointed out the dramatic and operatic quality of his paintings.

Dana L. Thomas observed that in William's work, "color is the expression of the poet giving the ultimate persuasiveness to the message of the philosopher."

William's love of music was inevitably an integral element of his art. He not only sang but also was a gifted musician, able to play several instruments. He read music and could transpose it, and his sense of pitch was perfect. He admired Bach as a musical architect and incorporated Bach's feeling for sweeping design into his own work. William linked art with music and gave his work a rhythmic, tonal dimension that lifted it above the purely visual state.

William was fond of painting chamber music groups and classical music subjects. He depicted not only the figures playing the instruments but also the rhythm of the music itself. The violin, viola, and cello radiated their own individual tone colors. The violin had a golden brown or reddish tone that seemed to float through the air as if the sound was moving out of the picture into the viewer's mind.

Once William used an accordion player as his model. The musician was so intrigued by the painting, he told him, "I'm willing to give you my week's salary to buy it."

William also loved dance. In the chorus of the Metropolitan Opera he had observed the ballets. In Spain he did a glowing painting of a flamenco dance group. He was also inspired by ballerinas when he visited Paris. Throughout his career, William kept returning to the theme of the dance. Sometimes he drew dancers in a pas de deux. Sometimes the dancers were in Russian folk costume. In his later works, the dancers became increasingly abstract to the point, finally, where only the rhythms of the dance itself were felt.

From the beginning, William's purpose was to underline and emphasize movement, not only in his dancers but in his other work. One of the most salient features of his widely popular paintings of horses was their rhythm and movement. Central to his philosophy as an artist was the importance of *motion* in a painting. The eye of the onlooker, William knew, is swift enough to instantly grasp the dynamics of motion in viewing the totality of a work. Even in his still lifes and landscapes he captured the qualities of movement and rhythm. One study I especially cherish, which is hanging in the Phillips Museum in Washington, was done at Folly Cove. It is a study of a cantaloupe and several peaches, against a background of drapery. One can feel that a breeze is wafting in from the sea; the porpoises are playing and spraying great fountains of water on a clear summer day.

William was particularly skillful in painting drapery. Titian used drapery as a curtain to show off his nudes. Rembrandt's drapery was frequently adorned with pearls or other precious jewels. Cézanne's drapery was part of the rigid foundation of his cubic form; he made his stark assertions with heavily loaded brushes, putting the colors on layer by layer. In William's paintings, the draperies were soft and yielding, subject to change with the lilt of the wind.

William knew how to develop the line of the tree to convey the feel of growth below the surface and of the extending branches. We had the "Meyerowitz Tree" that he painted frequently, with the harbor in the distance, the sloping hill, which the children traversed on the way to school, their figures getting smaller as they disappeared behind the rocks. William's tree had a majesty, shielding us from the sun and offering a benediction.

A number of William's landscapes were of Manhattan skyscrapers, for he was as fascinated with the city as the countryside. He said,

> I think of New York skyscrapers as stalagmites in a cave; as if they were not man-made phenomena, but a natural outgrowth of time. They plow into the earth as powerfully as they tower above the ground. A building is like a tree that is planted into the earth. New York is almost solid bedrock and I try to convey this quality as the great buildings rise out of

their concrete. I try to express a powerful cubic sense without making it too stark; to convey solidity paradoxically soaring into the atmosphere, breaking above the clouds, and sometimes balanced against the sun.

Critics sometimes likened William's work to that of Cézanne. Probably it was because they both studied nature so comprehensively. Cézanne used the cone, the sphere, and the cube as his means for expressing nature. William conveyed the dynamic relationship between the forms. The tree clutched the ground exuberantly as it soared upward. In his landscapes, William became more and more abstract as time went on. This was not only apparent in his later color etchings but also in his oils.

William was not averse to painting portraits, but he refused to serve a sitter's vanity. He refused to be beholden to a patron, and for this reason he did not accept many portrait commissions. He chose voluntarily the individual he wished to paint. He never felt comfortable with the prospect of portraying people unless he became personally acquainted with them and came to understand their personalities, a process that had to be based on more than a superficial introduction.

William painted himself frequently, sitting on a bench in his garden or working in the studio. On one occasion he did a portrait of himself enveloped in the folds of a prayer shawl with only his face emerging.

In his early and middle years, William painted his horses generally in the foreground. The younger ones looked at the older ones, the slower ones at the faster ones. Some-

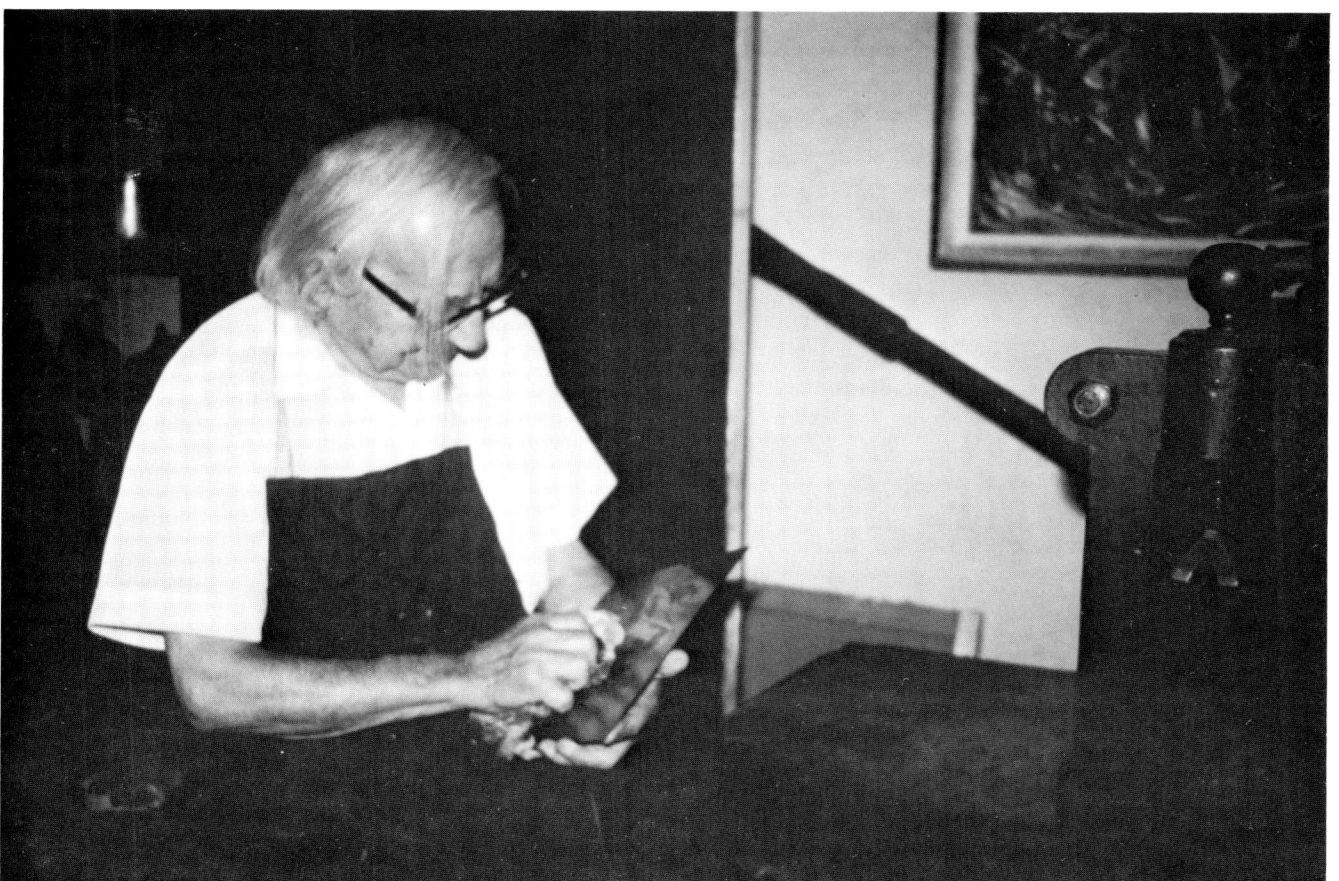

William Printing, 1978, photo by Marilyn Clark

times they glanced back at the ones behind them. There is a feeling that the horses are dancing a scherzo. Once, in a burst of humor, William painted himself as a clown sitting astride a horse and playing a violin. Every aspect of the horse fascinated him. He caught them galloping, trotting, and cantering. He painted the horses of Sanbateum, which were said to be the steeds of the lost tribes of Israel. William turned more and more to symbolism. He moved from the park, into realms of fancy, levitating his animals into the empyrean atmosphere in which they danced like musical notes from the harp. The titles of his works suggest their variety—*The Chase, The Path Finders, Horses of the Golden West, The Horseback Riders, Fantastic Horses, Race Horses, Legendary Horses,* and *Medieval Horses.* Following a series of horses of the American Wild West, William did a series called, "Horses in the Sky," which were fantasies played out in space.

Once in our younger days when we were struggling to make ends meet, William received a phone call from a man who announced, "I want two paintings of your horses to hang on each side of my fireplace."

The man insisted that he was coming over to the studio.

William went through his paintings and found a canvas of horses that was nearly square. He took a saw and cut it in two. I was stunned. I said, "Must you do this?"

"I've got to see," he replied calmly.

William puttered around with his brush and touched up the paintings. One group of horses went off toward the distance; the other group moved toward the foreground. They balanced each other splendidly.

When the buyer arrived, he chirped, "I knew you'd find me some paintings!"

Another genre that became a Meyerowitz trademark is his religious paintings and etchings. William had a profound empathy with the themes of the immigrant and with Hebraic motifs. He made the pilgrimage from Eastern Europe to America. He often said he had been born twice. He had been born in Russia and lived his childhood in the Ukraine. When he emigrated to the United States, he was born again. When, as an art student in Manhattan, he etched the immigrants sitting on a park bench, or old men studying the Bible in the Synagogue, William realized how lucky he and they were to be able to live their lives without fear of persecution in this land of the free.

When William sketched in the synagogue, he would conceal his pad under a prayer shawl. One day one of the elders upbraided him. "You don't seem to be looking at your book. You're always watching us. We wonder whether you can even read the prayers."

William took up his book and commenced reciting in Hebrew one of the most difficult passages.

The elders said, "*Gonif* (Fraud), we don't know what to make of you. People have spent years trying to learn these prayers."

Once William gained their confidence, they went about their daily praying and discussions. He produced *The Talmudists* and *The Discussion.* Another popular work in this genre was *The Rooster and the Book.* This study represented personal sacrifice. In biblical times, the Jews sacrificed in the temple, offering a goat or some other prized possession as a sign of their devotion to God. Marc Chagall painted goats. For William, the rooster symbolized the awakening of the day, the coming of light, and the orthodox tradition. The "Book" symbolized the spiritual and creative life of the Jews; hence, *The Rooster and the Book.*

William also made several paintings and etchings of *Moses* holding the tablets. First, there were only nine Commandments. Then Moses found the people worshiping the Golden Calf. It had been made from the jewelry that Aaron, the brother of Moses, had melted in his foundry. When Moses witnessed this scene, he dashed the nine Com-

William, by Peter A. Juley & Son

mandments to the ground. He returned to Mount Sinai, and carved the tenth Commandment: Thou shalt not worship a graven image.

William painted the prophet *Jeremiah* and the scenes of the *High Holidays*. He did the large *Synagogue of the Ari,* a tenth-century structure in Safed where the Kabbalah was founded by Rabbi Shimon Ba Yahai. And he did studies of humble Jews of the present. He did one subject of a grandfather listening to his grandson playing the violin. It was a Jewish tradition that some member of the family had to play the violin. There was a unique feeling of hope imparted by the music of this instrument, as reflected in *The Fiddler on the Roof.*

William kept coming back to his study of the *Exodus,* depicting Jews walking out of the darkness of persecution groping toward a better life, bringing the Torah and their talents and labor. He etched and painted several "Crucifixions." He observed that the Jews as a whole, like Christ, have been crucified, not once, but continually through the ages. In the 1940s, William made several paintings of the *Holocaust,* and he depicted the *Three Dictators*—Hitler, Mussolini, and Stalin—who heaped so much misery on mankind.

ETCHING

The process of etching involves the eating out, with acid on a copper plate, the forms that the artist desires to print. William's etching included works in black and white, as well as etchings in color.

He acquired his printing press at a very early stage in his career when he was living with his family on 120th Street. He worked with the same press throughout his life. It is still in our studio in Gloucester. This printing press had seen service in an entirely different role before it belonged to him. It had been used in the U.S. Mint for proofing, and later the U.S. Treasury sold it. A collector gave it to William as a gift. It had a very heavy spike wheel that William turned to get the metal plates to produce the prints. He knew just exactly how much pressure to exert on the little slabs of metal in order to get the quality of impression he desired; how to apply the blotters—sometimes one, sometimes two—to produce an extra heavy pressure on the plate. Rembrandt had etched his plates in stages. William etched most of his plates in a single stage, so they were all, in a very literal sense, first-edition etchings.

THE FOX FILM COMPANY

When William first introduced his etchings, they made important news in the art world. In 1925 the Fox Film Company was going to produce a documentary film showing the process of etching. The producers had been searching for a suitable artist who could etch directly on the plate in the film. They made inquiries from the dealers on Madison Avenue, who said that William could do this. When he was asked, William said that he was very willing to make the film. It was shot at the Hotel des Artistes, with illumination from four smoky klieg lights. The filmmakers had some initial reservations about the subject, fearing that it might not be interesting enough to a wide public. But, even as William was making the etching, the workmen on the crew were so absorbed in watching him that they forgot to load the film into the camera. The whole thing had to be shot over again. This was a black-and-white film, and the etching was black and white. It was one of the last films made during the silent era. The subject of the etching was a beautiful ballerina, posed by Madge Quimby from the Ziegfield Follies. William's printing press had been moved from the 120th Street apartment to the Hotel des Artistes for the movie. Afterwards, he had it shipped to Gloucester.

When the movie was finished, the producers called it *The Magic Needle*. The premiere showing was given in the Fox Studio building on 10th Avenue, with many of their stars attending, including Cary Grant and Dorothy and Lillian Gish. The film had wide distribution in moviehouses.

ETCHING IN COLOR

William was among the foremost practitioners of etching in color. It had been the dream of every etcher since Rembrandt to realize the life of an etching in color. Many experiments since the early Dutchman's were made with the hope of depicting the beauty of nature through this medium. Inks of a warm brown quality and creamy paper were developed, and subsequently a red or burnt sienna color was used by French and English etchers. Whistler achieved a brilliant new effect by using greenish paper and ink in his moonlight series.

William's draftsmanship had nobility. He etched over a thousand plates made with only a few impressions each. He did not concentrate on printing large editions. Everything from a Meyerowitz etching was printed by the artist himself. William did not have an assistant, and he did not rely on outside printers as did most etchers, including Joseph Pennell, Whistler, and Edward Hopper. Even Picasso and Matisse had their plates touched up and finished by outside printers. Only during the final months of his life did William finally permit somebody else to turn the great spike wheel of his printing press for him. Throughout his career William mixed his own inks. He used to take yellows, a dash of red—the Indian or Venetian red—the ochres, the sienna, and sometimes the permanent blues—and mix them individually with stand oil until they were a very fine grain.

For William, to etch was as personal as to compose a letter in his own handwriting. He communicated his emotions, ideas, and artistic decisions through the rigid medium of copper or zinc, which could not easily be altered or transformed, handling them with the intimacy and flexibility a successful etching requires. William conquered the intractability of the metal plate with the obsessiveness of Captain Ahab pursuing the White Whale. He superimposed yellows with reds to produce a mysterious quality and put just enough blue on to provide an element of tragedy and darkness—thus producing the balance of sunlight and moonlight that made his work compelling.

He had a feeling for the abstract on a miniature scale. Most abstractions by artists are done on large surfaces to give scope and vent to their talent for color formation. William worked in miniature with delicate nuances of colors merging into one another.

William used subtle techniques. Sometimes after he applied a batch of ink to a plate with a soft leather roller, he would start wiping it off with a blotter rolled up to a fine point. With his fingers and a bit of talcum powder, he would start polishing off the very light parts of the plate; for instance, a white sail, the shirt of a fisherman, the edge of a cloud in the sky. He had a special passion for an earthy green—like the color of grass absorbing the sun's rays, a touch of metallic yellow flashing like lightning.

William's first etchings were of people and scenes of New York. Then he made scenes of Ridgefield, and then of Gloucester. His etchings of the harbor became bolder in color as he evolved his ideas. As his artistic vision became increasingly sophisticated, William developed a technique of making a print in various colors by using several plates. He drilled holes into the plates so that he could put the paper back in the same register. In the prints by Pissarro, one clearly sees the different colors that were mixed, since they were not in the same register. William succeeded in overcoming this defect. When the Boston Museum of Fine Arts acquired one of William's etchings in color, it also purchased a Pissarro etching to demonstrate to students the advances made in the technique.

At the Hale studio at Folly Cove, William continued experimenting with color. He strove to gain certain effects by superimposing one color over another on one plate, or with two plates, or in three printings, according to his concept.

THE PROCESS OF PRINTING

Etching comes from the Dutch word *etzen* meaning to eat out.

It is preferable that the etching plate be made of copper, and be either 16 or 18 gage in thickness. A zinc plate can be used, but the only advantage that zinc has over copper is that it bites a little faster because it's a softer metal. William made his own etching materials—the balls of beeswax, burgundy pitch, and asphaltum. He put these three ingredients together, boiled them in a little iron container on a very small flame until they melted, then he'd cool the mix, scrape it out, and roll it into a small ball the size of a plum. He took some taffeta silk from an old umbrella, cut a square, put the little ball inside the square piece of taffeta, and tied it up with a strong thread. He heated the plate, holding it with a clamp handle over a candle flame for a short while. When it was warm he would rub the ball gently over the surface in order to relase the wax through the silk. Then it had to be rolled, spreading the warm wax all over the plate. Next it had to be blackened with a lit taper, passing it up and down, back and forth over the surface of the plate, until it was completely sooted. This gave the surface a uniform black background. When it was perfectly dry, he would put the plate into a photographic holder to make it easier to work on. He would go outside and start drawing on the plate with a needle in a holder, in such a way that every line would be revealed. If he held it against the light, he could see the sparkle of the line. As the little Italian boys used to say when they watched us work in Venice, *"Ponte d'oro,"* meaning, "A golden point!" After William finished his drawing, he would use stove enamel to cover the back of the plate and the edges, to protect the plate from the acid.

When the plate was ready, he would place it in an acid bath, six parts of water, and one part of nitric acid, forming a very powerful acid. Sometimes he would test the bath by putting a copper penny into it and watching it smoke. Then he would lower the plate into it and with a feather he would push away the bubbles from each line. And the lines would become as firm and as deep as he desired to have them. Then he took the plate out of the acid. If he wanted a very dark line, he might bite it for sixty minutes. If he wanted a very light line, he would take it out in fifteen or twenty minutes and cover that line. In that way, he would get the proper color contrasts in his picture and the proper foreground and distance. He would take the lines that he did not wish to have exposed in the acid, dip it into water and blot it off, then cover the light lines with the enamel. He would put the plate back into the acid again to cut the darker lines. This procedure would go on for three or four sessions. When he was completely finished with the biting, he would take it out and clean off the surface carefully with turpentine or benzene. It is necessary to be very careful. The plate would then be ready for printing. He used a solid etching ink, and he warmed the plate a little on a kerosene stove to dissolve the thickness of the ink. He quickly wiped the ink over the plate in circular fashion. He would wipe it until he was satisfied that the ink was in the line and not too much on the surface of the plate. Then he would get his paper ready, a vellum, or silk rag paper of English origin, with a surface that was not too absorbent.

For aquatint, William used a big box covered with a wire sieve. Powdered resin was placed on the sieve and the plate was in the box. With a blow of a hammer, the resin would land on the plate. For light spots, he would cover them with some enamel. The rest of the plate would be bitten into aquatint. Then he would place the plate in the nitric acid. William took away the light parts, such as clouds in the sky or the silhouette of a building or the reflection of the water or the roof of a housetop, by covering them with enamel. He would bite this in the acid to get a contrast between the dark, the halftone, and the light. The light might be almost without any powder on it, with just a slight tonality. He would proof it by inking the plate and putting it through the press with a dampened paper. The paper generally was dampened the night before. He blotted the paper to absorb excessive moisture just before printing.

He would make a proof, then ink the plate, then put the plate back into the press, and pull the damp proof over the surface. Then he would pull the large spike wheel of the press and he would have his first impression of the etching. As our friend, Ellen Day Hale, would say, "Truly the etching was born in the press."

William filled one closet to the brim with his finished plates, packed in brown paper. In the early days he wrote the titles out in longhand, but later on he no longer had the time to classify every single one of his works. Some of his most important plates are still stored in the closet. He was a master printer. The plates have subsequently been classified by William's nephew, Keith Carlson, and myself.

Meyerowitz's subject matter can be divided into several groupings. His early motifs were of the people on New York's Lower East Side. He could read in their faces the character of their ancestry. He felt the agitation, isolation, and expectation in the eyes of the immigrants. Then later on, when he etched the buildings of New York City, he devoted himself to transmitting the aspirations of a growing, vibrating metropolis in which immigrants from many nations lived side by side in harmony.

He etched scenes of Gloucester, which is over three hundred fifty years old. He caught the moods and activities of the Gloucester fishermen, who are mostly Portuguese and Italian, and who continue to live and practice the customs of their heritage. The annual festival of their patron, Saint Peter, is still held every year. He etched them as they sat on the dock cross-legged like tailors, manipulating their bobbins to and fro to mend the torn edges of their nets so that the fish would not escape capture on the next trip.

He etched other craftsmen, particularly musicians playing their instruments. For instance, he did an etching of a cellist, with his instrument held between his knees, his head bent over as he clutched the bow and played the strings that gave forth a thrilling lyricism.

William etched a number of self-portraits. They included some in color, others in black and white, some on large plates, and others quite small. There were several double portraits in which we were depicted together.

He labeled his etchings, as well as his paintings, in a direct fashion. For William, sunset was sunset; Gloucester Harbor was just that. The Exodus was entitled, simply, *Exodus*.

To behold the etchings of old Hebrew and Hasidic subjects is to be drawn into an aesthetic world. The Hasidim, whom he etched in Jerusalem, danced or prayed at sunrise. Even as they studied they would shake from side to side and move backwards

Theresa, 1982, by Daniel Salo

William Meyerowitz

and forward in rhythm to their incantations. This is the expression of the "Tropp"—the rhythmic cadence of the Hebrew prayer. In some of William's etchings in this genre—*The High Holiday, The Idealist, The Chasidim*—there is a mood reminiscent of Rembrandt. Many people have remarked about this. William was an artist who was able to express the serenity of centuries earlier, when religious faith was the lodestone of individual and social conduct, and the spiritual mission of the human race was an ideal to be achieved.

Some of William's first etchings found their way into collections. One was the collection of Lessing Rosenwald. It included works by Albert Dürer, Rembrandt, and Meyerowitz and is now in the National Gallery.

Mr. Rosenwald, the head of the Sears Roebuck Company, invited us to see his collection in Germantown, Pennsylvania, where he had his headquarters. He showed William two prints by Dürer on the same subject.

"Which is the original?"

William pointed to one of them.

Then Rosenwald took me into the room and asked me the same question. I pointed to the one I believed was the original. It turned out that both prints were from the same plate, but one had been made much earlier and the second was done much later. Both William and I had selected the original.

"How did you know?" Rosenwald asked.

"I studied the lines," William replied, "and I knew where lines had been added to improve the condition of the plate."

I told him the same thing.

He was very satisfied. "You both know your field."

Art critics and writers analyzed his work, such as Royal Cortissoz, Dana Thomas, and Agnes Delano, cousin of Franklin Delano Roosevelt.

Dr. Henry Thomas, author of *Biographies of Famous Artists*, wrote the following:

> William Meyerowitz loved humanity and painted the simple events about him, shaping the forms in color as a sculptor shapes them out of clay. Youth, motherhood, and old age interested him and Nature became his great adventure. Trees and rocks spoke to him of a rhythm and a subtle harmony, which he incorporated into his works. He was compared to Cézanne before he knew who Cézanne was. Still, it might have been said that Rembrandt and St. Francis were his inspirations. To each of them Nature revealed a great secret, a spiritual elixir, which made it possible for them and for chosen men and women of all generations to find and taste the fruit thereof.

Although William suffered a heart attack in 1961, it did not deter him from continuing the journey of exploration into the pathways of his artistic realm. He continued to work for the next twenty years, until the final months of his life.

The last summer we spent in Gloucester, William produced some of his most exuberant works, among them, *The Large Garden, Horses in the Sky,* and *The Abandoned House.*

His brush had become even more airy as it danced over the canvas. His horses floated through space like butterflies. The house he painted—an abandoned one to the rear of our garden—seemed to be the very apotheosis of all houses haunted by old memories. His very last work involved retouching and embellishing a portrait he had previously done of me—one of his favorite paintings. The devotion he lavished on this portrait in his final days has served as a testament of all the love he felt for me.

And so we lay in the early morning light, his sheltering arm beneath my back. It was the way he always held me as we confronted the world together.

"To be forever in your embrace," I whispered.

Appendix A
One-Man Exhibitions

1919	Milch Gallery, New York City
1920	Milch Gallery, New York City
	Concord Art Association, Concord, Mass.
1921	Corcoran Gallery of Art, Washington, D.C.
	Syracuse Museum of Fine Arts, Syracuse, N.Y.
1923	Irving & Casson, Boston, Mass.
	A. H. Davenport, Boston, Mass.
	National Museum, Smithsonian Institute, Washington, D.C.
1924	Milch Gallery, New York City
1926	Milch Gallery, New York City
	Vassar College, Poughkeepsie, N.Y.
1927	Civic Club, New York City
1928	Doll & Richards, Boston, Mass.
1929	Kraushaar Art Gallery, New York City
	Kleeman Thorman Gallery, New York City
1930	Baltimore Museum of Art, Baltimore, Md.
	Dayton Art Institute, Dayton, Ohio
	Corcoran Gallery of Art, Washington, D.C.
1931	Barbizon Plaza Art Gallery, New York City
	Maryland Institute of Art, Baltimore, Md.
1932	Albany Institute of Art, Albany, N.Y.
	Arnot Art Gallery, Elmira, N.Y.
	Utica Public Library, Utica, N.Y.
1933	Boston City Club, Boston, Mass.
1935	Brooks Memorial Art Gallery, Memphis, Tenn.
1936	Dayton Art Institute, Dayton, Ohio
	Columbus Gallery of Fine Arts, Columbus, Ohio
	The John Herron Art Institute, Indianapolis, Ind.
	Fort Wayne Art School and Museum, Fort Wayne, Ind.
1937	University of Nebraska, Lincoln, Neb.
1938	The Print Club, Albany, N.Y.
1940	Findlay Galleries, Chicago, Ill.
	Uptown Gallery, New York City

1941	Robert C. Vose Gallery, Boston, Mass.
1941–42	National Museum, Smithsonian Institute, Washington, D.C.
1942	Currier Gallery of Art, Manchester, N.H.
1943	American British Art Center, New York City
1944	Grace Horne Art Gallery, Boston, Mass.
	Museum of Society of State Teachers, Potsdam, N.Y.
1945	American British Art Center, New York City
1946	American British Art Center, New York City
	Michigan State University, East Lansing, Mich.
1947	Doll & Richards, Boston, Mass.
	American British Museum, New York City
	University of Nebraska, Lincoln, Nebraska
1948	American British Art Center, New York City
1949	Doll and Richards, Boston, Mass.
	Public House, Sturbridge, Mass.
1950	New Brunswick Art Center, New Brunswick, N.J.
1951	Doll and Richards, Boston, Mass.
1953	Doll and Richards, Boston, Mass.
1955	Schoneman Gallery, New York City
1956	Carus Gallery, New York City
1957	Chase Gallery, New York City
1959	Chase Gallery, New York City
	Park Gallery, Detroit, Mich.
1960	University of Maine, Orono, Me.
1961	Park Gallery, Detroit, Mich.
	Moniss Gallery, Detroit, Mich.
1965	Chase Gallery, New York City
1966	Bar Harbor Art Gallery, Bar Harbor, Me.
	Columbus Museum Art Gallery, Columbus, Ga.
	University of Georgia, Athens, Ga.
	Athens Art Museum, Athens, Ga.
	Carus Gallery, New York City
1967	Columbus Museum Art Gallery, Columbus, Ga.
1968	Gainesville Art Association, Gainesville, Fla.
	Montgomery Museum of Fine Arts, Montgomery, Ala.
	Chase Art Gallery, New York City
1972	Chase Art Gallery, New York City
1974	Butler Art Institute, Youngstown, Ohio
1975	Harvard Law School, Cambridge, Mass.
1976	Smith-Girard, Stamford, Conn.
	Sawyer Library, Gloucester, Mass.
1977	Summit Gallery, New York City
1979	Summit Gallery, New York City
1982	Bethesda Gallery, Bethesda, Maryland
1983	Cayuga Museum of History and Art, Auburn, New York
	Rockport Art Association, Rockport, Massachusetts
1983–84	The New-York Historical Society, New York City
1984	Patterson Public Library, Patterson, New Jersey

Appendix B
Permanent Collections and Awards

*WILLIAM MEYEROWITZ IS REPRESENTED IN
THE PERMANENT COLLECTION OF:*

U.S. National Museum, Smithsonian Institution; Metropolitan Museum of Art; Phillips Memorial Art Gallery, Washington, D.C.; Boston Museum of Fine Arts; Concord Arts Association; The Cone Collection; Brooklyn Museum of Fine Arts; Bibliothèque Nationale, Paris; Library of Congress, Washington, D.C.; Museum of Modern Art; New York Public Library; Albany Institute of Arts and History; Harvard Club, New York; John Herron Art Institute; Speed Memorial Art Gallery; Brandeis University; Yale University; University of Kentucky; the Currier Gallery of Art; Fitchburg Art Museum; Ein Harod Museum; Bezalel Museum, Jerusalem; Tel Aviv Museum; Univeristy of Maine, Orono, Maine; Columbus Museum of Art, Columbus, Georgia; University of Georgia, Athens Museum of Art; Montgomery Museum of Art, Montgomery, Alabama; Terra Museum, Evanston, Illinois; The Museum of American Art, National Museum, Washington, D.C.; George Washington University; City College of New York; and many private collections.

AWARDS

1916	Prix de Rome—"Drama as a Teacher"
1918	National Academy of Design—NY—1st Prize in drawing, painting & etching
1939	First Prize for painting "Gloucester Harbor," Shore Arts Association
1939	Modern Contemporary Painters Prize for Painting "Exodus"
1950	Library of Congress for Etching
1950	First Prize for Etching in Color: American Color Print Society
1950	Popular Prize for Painting "Gloucester St.," Cape Ann Society of Modern Artists
1956	Anonymous Prize Audubon Society of Art for Painting "Still Life"
1957	First Prize for Painting "Still Life Window," North Shore Arts Association
1958	The Shore Prize & Citation, Audubon Society of Artists
1958	The Clair Layton Prize for Painting "Horseback Rider," Audubon Society of Artists

1959	Seton Hall University Gold Key
1960	Prize for Painting, Allied Artists of America
1961	Rockport Art Association First Prize for Painting "Panel Fantasy"
1963	Honorable Mention for Portrait, Rockport Art Association
1965	W. F. Schrafft Award for Best Painting in the Exhibition "Horseback Riders," Rockport, Massachusetts
1965	Speyer Prize for Painting "The Chase," National Academy of Design
1965	The Vayana Prize for Painting "Musician," Art Center, Ogunquit, Maine
1966	The Grumbacher Purchase Prize, Audubon Artists, New York
1967	Honorable Mention, Ogunquit Art Center
1968	The Hatfield Art Prize for Painting, Rockport Art Association
1969	The North Shore Arts Memorial Award for Painting "Equestrians"
1969	Etching Prize, Rockport Art Association
1969	The Carl R. Matson Prize for Portrait, Rockport Art Association
1970	The Gold Medal of Honor, Rockport Art Association
1978	Gold Medal of Honor, Rockport Art Association
1979	Allied Artists—Salmagundi Award
1980	Gold Medal, Honorary Member—Italian Academy of Art, Parma, Italy
1983	Academico de Europe International Exhibition for Peace, Palazzo, Parma, Italy (awarded posthumously)

Appendix C
Excerpts from Commentaries on the
Works of William Meyerowitz
(1925–1980)

WILLIAM MEYEROWITZ HAS ALWAYS DISPLAYED, WITH SOUND CRAFTSMANSHIP AND trained observation, a swift perception of the emotional key in which his creative reassembling of objective fact was to be set. His newest technical innovation is in color etching, in which, by an elaborate process of superimposed pigments, he obtains three-dimensional design with both the precision of lineal design and the charm of colors of pastel painting. In such a plate as *Trees,* the most imperceptible of color transitions builds up palpable forms: there is an effect of depth and space between the solidly rooted trees that surprises one. The glowing *Autumn Hills,* with its gamut of russet tones, or the flushed sky and water of *Gloucester Evening,* must go on record in an exhibition which has many facets of interest and many emotional appeals in its apparent simplicity of direct record.

—Margaret Breuning
New York Post

William Meyerowitz's exhibition of etchings in color is drawing fresh attention to an artist whose work has been steadily progressing. Although, not new enough to have escaped the watchful eyes of collectors who have lent many of the items for this occasion. It is highly impressive work. Not only does it carry the charm of fine etching but it is also endowed with a quality of color treatment that a painter's touch can convey. There is no one more envied in his era than an artist who can be acclaimed as a painter and etcher. It is a distinction few attain, although many aspire to it. Something more than facility in changing a brush for a needle is essential. These etchings in color show the deep artistic feeling.

—F. W. Eddy

William Meyerowitz is not a sensationalist and does not paint with the idea of causing confusion and doubt as to his message. He finds beauty, peace and tranquility in the world around him and his simple aim is to share it with you.

—Herbert Chase
Chase Gallery, N.Y.

William Meyerowitz has the secret of self-renewing youthful zest in his work, at the same time growing in strength. In reviewing the work of William Meyerowitz it seems to me to be the most felicitous group of paintings I have ever seen.

These paintings reveal a versatility not only in range of mediums employed, but also in the variety of approaches to the subject. What Meyerowitz conceives in a light spirit is expressed with a corresponding lightness of touch: and where the subject is sombre, the style takes on deeper sonorities of tone and form, his color is fresh, the designs of his compositions are spirited.

The recent paintings by William Meyerowitz include his newest landscapes done in a luminously prismatic manner in which shafts of light subtly dart over the panorama and work atmospheric magic with the houses, trees and sky.

Light on the Harbor is eminently successful in this vein. Other high spots are *Trees in Rhythm, Street in Safed* and the large still life which was awarded the Audubon Artists Prize recently in New York.

—Charles Z. Offin
Pictures On Exhibit

Drawing plays an important part in the paintings by William Meyerowitz. Unlike many painters with a free and skillful technique, Meyerowitz uses abstract form and cubist organization for his new effects. The results are fresh, natural and radiant in color.

—Carlyle Burrows
N. Y. Herald Tribune

William Meyerowitz has been identified with modern American art for many years. In the medium of paint as well as etching, he displays a concentrated devotion both to craftsmanship and idea.

Meyerowitz concentrates upon the inner structural design, painting what he beholds to be essential. He is not an abstract artist, although he employs certain devices of abstraction to strengthen design and to achieve clarification. He uses his colors economically but forcefully. He maintains a mood which is seldom found, a mood of cheerfulness and lyricism. He is personal in expression and unafraid of sentimentality.

Among his pictures are landscapes, symbolic subjects, studies of equestrians, and some genre. There is variety in his paintings, and everything he undertakes has character and interest.

—Dorothy Adlow
The Christian Science Monitor

William Meyerowitz's paintings probe into the heart of things.

—Dana Thomas
Living Biographies of Great Painters

William Meyerowitz, an American-trained artist, has been pursuing his art with a single minded intensity. Amidst the clamor and contention he has kept the even tenor of his way; his form of painting cannot be catalogued as traditional, primitive or abstract; they have the validity of reflecting simply and wholeheartedly his own view of life, undistorted by any other consideration. They are paintings that probe into the heart of things.

Meyerowitz strives in his work for the structural logic beneath the mere ripple of atmosphere light. He searches for the essential structural ideas that had existed in eternity. He does not paint merely what eye sees, but the underlying order of form that the intellect comprehends.

The philosophy suggested by Meyerowitz in his structural form is the artist's saying that nothing in nature is created except from a fundamental archetype.

The key that Meyerowitz uses to unlock his kingdom of eternal reality and lure the viewer to visit with him is his ravishing employment of color. Color is the expression of the poet, giving the ultimate persuasiveness to the message of the philosopher.

The range and delicacy of Meyerowitz's colors are impressive. Harnessed to the archetypal stability of his forms, they represent the poignancy of time's ephemeral nature, worn like an alluring cosmetic on the face of the everlasting.

He has been a lifelong explorer of the mystery and mysticism of color. Indeed, he is a pioneer in the development of printing etchings in color from the plate. His work in this field has become widely known.

Through the medium of his art, he has been able to fuse the sensibility of the architect with the finesse of a colorist into a single wholly convincing vision of life.

Meyerowitz's subjects are the panorama of life about him. They range from musical themes—he was a musician by nature—to the rhythmic movement of horses, trees, dancers, arrangements of fruit, flowers and draperies. From his home in Gloucester he looks out beyond the breakwater of earthly existence and audaciously casts the bark of his inspiration on a perpetual voyage of artistic exploration. It is the salt air of the sea that has quickened his spirit and kept him so young in the pursuit of his goals.

—Dana Thomas
Catalogue, Chase Gallery

William Meyerowitz, in his new watercolors and oils, seems to me to contribute to our serious productions of American painting the characteristics peculiar to the Slavic temperament—and for which I loved my Russian friends of academic days: suavity, together with that peculiar mystical complexity of many semi-Oriental strains and historical inbreedings. His innate musical bent is expressed by the delicacy of altering and vibrating the color-tones. A social tolerance, born from the destruction of tyrannical conventionalities, appears here as a sort of "clean sheet," as the light of paper or the airspace of blank canvas; a socially constructive sympathy that weaves together those unusual elements into a new and harmonious whole; with sensitive intellect he qualifies to the utmost each boundary line.

With such traits of soul his paintings always manifest a subtle aesthetic charm.

—Oscar Bluemner
Catalogue (1929), Kraushaar Gallery

William Meyerowitz is still faithful to Gloucester, and his tributes in paint to that port lack nothing of their early enthusiasm. In fact they increase upon it.

The part of town that fascinates him is the famous waterfront. His version of the ships and wharves are artistic enough to please the most ardent art connoisseurs.

What Meyerowitz admires above everything else is crispness of statement, as is evidently seen by the clear touches to be discovered in his paintings.

He is a clear-eyed painter susceptible to rhythms and is sensitively capturing them.

The paintings of Rabbis and Torahs are surprising and impressive.

The work by William Meyerowitz is lifted by some rapturous excitement into the lyrical realms of pure feeling. It has the fervor of worship which is the way good artists do their painting.

—Henry McBride
N.Y. Herald Tribune

Mr. Meyerowitz strikes a new, individualized note.
He is painterlike in his effects but not forgetful of the essential character of his art.
These are true etchings in color, the fruit of a technical process beautifully mastered.

—Royal Cortissoz
N.Y. Herald Tribune

The room in which these impressions are hung glows with enchanting loveliness, that has no peer in this form of art, among its contemporary practitioners. Especially fine are the prints—*Autumn Hills, The Trees*, portrait of *Ralph Cross Johnson, Justice Holmes, The Land's End*, and the noble *Patriarch*. It is a pleasure to see so delicate and flowerlike a technique as is this of color etching carried to such a pitch of high perfection as it is at the hands of Mr. Meyerowitz.

—W. B. McCormick

William Meyerowitz is American in art education and art impulses. His work exhibits an individualistic point of view particularly in his interpretation of American landscapes.

—C. J. Bulliet
Chicago

William Meyerowitz is a painter and an etcher. He received his first instruction at the National Academy of Design and has won numerous prizes in both etchings and paintings. He has given much of his time to the making of etchings in color. His method is to etch the plates to receive the color and by super-imposing one color over another obtain a mellow richness of effect. The result is unique. The etcher is invariably doing his own printing. The entire process is very different from wood-blocks, lithography or silk screen.

Taking into consideration the diversity of ways in which any art medium can be used, and the variety in style as well as viewpoint of the artist, it is remarkable that a work which has been produced by one of special talent almost immediately, upon sight, manifests its worth. This is exemplified in the etchings of William Meyerowitz.

No sooner does one set eyes upon these prints than assurance is given that here are works of exceptional value. Not only is the medium used well, but the spirit is that of the genuine artist. One who has something to say and says it clearly with complete absorption in the theme and its transcription. This has to do with the intangible side of art which gives to all art both charm and lasting merit.

It must not be forgotten that Mr. Meyerowitz is an exceptionally skillful etcher. His plates printed in black ink are distinguished performances. Among the portraits are Chief Justice Stone and Justice Holmes and other Justices of the Supreme Court. The landscapes and figures, motives of New York and New England coast represent an excellent variety.

—Leila Mechlin
American Federation of Art

Every artist's life is a struggle with the Angel, or, perhaps, a rather adventurous embrace of the Universe. The painter, looking at the bare canvas before him, and at the

Image he yearns to catch and put down, always hopes that he will prevail in the end, and he speaks to his Image as Jacob did wrestling with the Stranger, "I will not let thee go, except thou bless me."

Be it the struggle, not of one night; but of a full earthly life, William Meyerowitz does not let the Image go until it has blessed him—and blessed all of us who are gathered to share in his victory.

—Alfred Werner
Catalogue, Chase Gallery

William Meyerowitz seems to be able to bring us closer to the emotions. Nature flows spontaneously through his work. Sky, verdure and water mirror the light of the sun and the play of the wind. How he does it, what it is he does to produce that effect on us, would be hard to define. Just as indefinable as the pulse beat of the universe in the Beethoven Fifth. Yet we all know it is there for all time in his work. A sort of quiet music of the spheres. A work of art has it, whatever it is, can never lose its charm though styles may change. This is the basic foundation upon which the bridge of beauty rests. Whatever the subject William Meyerowitz selects, it is the abstract quality to be found in his paintings that gives them their unusual fascination.

—Henry Thomas

William Meyerowitz is a good painter and a good etcher, and he knows well where to draw the line between the two kinds of art. His range is wide, from the intellectual charm and fervor of some of his heads, and the intense characterization of others, to his landscape work in all its phases—sometimes what is called pure landscape, of tree and plain. Different men and epochs in art cultivated different phases of perception, the literal or the abstract, the emotional or the rational. Surely the over-emphasis of the intellectual ingredient imperils the emotional balance of a work of art. It is a proof of sound artistic judgment in Meyerowitz that he knows how to render both, the emotional and the intellectual factors, subservient to artistic unity. The spiritual beauty he achieves has its source in this balance. This also supplies the perhaps subconscious motive for the rhythmic sonority of his line.

An etcher is no etcher unless he feels; and Meyerowitz's feeling is so personal, so strong, and so noble that that alone would give his work high rank. But he has the rest of the etcher's qualities too. Line, character, power of composition, power of suggesting that elusive thing, a crowd of people, with the simplest means—he has all these, and you feel that no other medium could express them so well. But, once more, you feel that all these things are informed by a steady flame of emotion—a lamp which not many artists trim and guard so well.

—Ellen Day Hale
Catalogue, Milch Gallery

William Meyerowitz's exhibition of etchings in color is giving visitors further opportunity to see this really beautiful work. It is informed throughout with a delicate spirit of artistry that shows itself thoroughly at home in a medium by no means over-exploited. The color is often haunting in its values that seem to underlie values, and the sense of design proves an apt confederate.

—Edward Alden Jewell
N.Y. Times

An article on Meyerowitz's art written by Charles Movalli appeared in the January 1980 issue of *American Artist* Magazine.

Appendix D
Comments by the Artist on His Work

I AM OFTEN ASKED THE QUESTION, "TO WHAT SCHOOL OF PAINTING DO YOU BELONG? MY answer is: "What does it matter?"

I have been a diligent pupil of the National Academy of Design, New York, and of the old masters. I have investigated old trends and all styles in art and have become a pupil of nature and of life about me. Intuition and common sense are my guidons. I am independent, bound by the tenets of no narrow academic association and prejudiced against no new discovery or movement. Form to me is the expression of things and form of life which we are enveloped in, inhaling the surroundings.

Painting, like music, poetry, or literature, is a universal language. It is created by the sensitive members of the society. The environment, the sensitivity of the artist, his search for the truth, create a personal expression of individuality in his work.

Because of my musical background, I enjoy painting musical subjects. Music in general evokes in me a sensation of warm colors, predominantly red and yellow.

As far back as I can remember, I made drawings of horses. Horseback riders in the park are giving me new ideas and fantasy for painting. I am painting abstract, semi-abstract, and postimpressionistic, depending on my esthetic sensibility or of the subject which it might suggest. Very often I lean toward a more objective representation because I find it to be a more suitable vehicle for the subtle pervasive harmonies and delicate modulation.

—William Meyerowitz
ca. 1964

Index

Amsterdam, 34–35
Assisi, 37
Atwood, William, 29

Babson, Roger, 40
Bakst, Leon, 38
Barrymore, John, 23, 47
Bellows, George, 9, 48
Ben-Gurion, David, 57, 70–71
Ben-Yehuda, Eliazer, 57, 70–71
Berlin, 35
Bernstein, Isadore, 44
Bernstein, Theresa: daughter of, 32; early art education of, 23–24; in Gloucester, 44; her life at Holbein Studios, 23; her marriage to William Meyerowitz and their studio on W. 67th Street, 26; photos of, 25, 82
Bluemner, Oscar, 73
Brandeis, Justice Louis, 61–62
Broun, Heywood, 47
Brumback, Judge, 40
Burluik, David, 48

Cardozo, Justice Benjamin, 62
Clemens, Gabrielle, 29, 30
Cone, Clarabel and Eta, 50–52
Cracow, 36
Cuernavaca, 66

Davis, Stuart, 39–40, 47
Demetrius, George, 30
de Sola Pool, Rabbi David, 57
Discussion, The (etching), 31–32, 58, 76
Duchamp, Marcel, 48

East Side, Lower, 17, 81
Einstein, Albert, 69–70; photo of, 41
Etching in color, 31, 79–80

Finnish colony, 30–32
Florence, 37
Folly Cove, 29–30, 80
Frankfurter, Justice Felix, 62
Friends of Zion, 10, 69

Gallery on the Moors, 29, 39
Gardner, Mrs. Jack, 28–29
Gezelitz (Ukrainian village), 13–15; as theme, 14
Glass, Joel, 58
Gloucester, scenes of, 29, 32, 81
Graefe, Julius Meier, 73

Haddad, Abraham, 39
Hales, the, 29–30; Ellen Day Hale, 29, 61, 80
Hancock, Walker, 30
Hassam, Childe, 29, 47
Hawthorne Inn (and casino), 28–29, 42
Hebraic themes, 15, 76, 78, 81, 84
Hellman, Lillian, 29
Hennessy, Mrs. Swan and Patrice, 54–56
Henri, Robert, 9
Hibbard, Aldro, 33
Higginson, Lee, 29
Holmes, Justice Oliver Wendell, 60–61
Hoover, Herbert, 64
Hopper, Edward, 48
Horses, as theme, 13, 74–76, 94
Hoyt, Margaret, 28, 30
Hurst, Fannie, 57

Immigrant themes, 76, 81

Javits, Jacob, 64
Jefferson Foundation, 9
Jerusalem, 71
Jewish Daily Forward, 56
Jewish Museum, 56
Johnson, Ralph Cross, 32

Karolik, Maxim, 59
Kollek, Teddy, 70
Kroll, Leon, 30
Kronberg, Lewis, 28

Lachaise, Gaston, 47, 50
La Guardia, Mayor Fiorello, 49
Landis, Dean, 62
Lipshitz, Jacques, 56–57
London, 34

Magic Needle, The (film), 78–79
Manship, Paul, 30
Marsh, Reginald, 46–47
Matisse, Henri, 51–52
Meir, Golda, 70
Metropolitan Opera, 19–21
Meyerowitz, Gershon, 13–14, 16–17, 21; photos of, 12, 21
Meyerowitz, Shendl, 14; photo of, 20; her samovar, 58; as subject, 22
Meyerowitz, William: his facility with languages, 20; his philosophy as artist, 74; photographic self-portraits by, 18, 19; photos of, 21, 25, 63, 68, 75, 77, 83; plants and paints the garden, 44–45; as singer, 19–20, 24; as teacher, 22
Mittelman, Menachem, 92
Mount Pleasant Avenue, house on, 39–42
Music, as theme, 74, 81

National Academy of Design, 18–19, 22, 73
Neagoe, Peter, 39
Nevelson, Louise, 53
Nobel (representative of firm), 15
North Shore Arts Association, 10, 29
Nyro, Laura, 59

O'Gorman, James, 31

Pach, Walter, 47
Paris, 38
Pene Du Bois, Guy, 47
People's Art Guild, 9
Pogrom, 14, 16
Printing, process of, 80

Rabin, Itzhak, 70
Ridgefield, N.J. art colony, 21–22, 26–27
Rivera, Diego, 65
Roberts, Justice Owen, 62, 64

Robinson, Mary Pomeroy, 53
Rockport Art Association, 33
Romano, Umberto, 48
Romney, Marie, 39
Rosenwald, Lessing, 84

Sargent, John Singer, 29
Sarnoff, David, 49, 53
Schiff, Jacob, 49
Shazar, Zalman, 70
Skyscrapers, as motif, 49, 74–75, 81
Sloan, John, 29, 47–48
Society of Independent Artists, 47–48
Soyer, Raphael, 48
Stern, Isaac, 48
Stone, Justice Harlan, 62
Strange, Michael, 23
Supreme Court Justices (Black, Douglas, Murphy), 62
Synagogues, Spanish and Portuguese, 57
Szold, Henrietta, 70

Taxco, 65–66
Tel Aviv, 72
Thomas, Dana, 73, 84
Thomas, Henry, 84
Tureck, Rosalyn, 59, 76

Vienna, 35

Warburg, Felix, 56
Waksman, Selman, 56
Weizmann, Chaim, 36, 69
Whitney, Gertrude, 46–47

Yiddish language, 17, 56

Zionists, 9, 69
Zorach, William, 47, 56

Chromatic Scale (1929)—Etching in Color—12″ × 10″—Collection Smith-Girard, Stamford, Conn.

Jacob's House, Gloucester (1933)—Watercolor—15″ × 19″—Collection Smith-Girard, Stamford, Conn.

Crucifixion (1929)—Etching in Color—10″ × 12″—Collection Smith-Girard, Stamford, Conn.

Fishermen Mending Nets (1942)—Oil—18″ × 25″—Collection Dr. & Mrs. Elton Yasona

Still Life with Iris (1940)—Etching in Color—8″ × 10″—Collection Metropolitan Museum of Art

Abstract Still Life (1947)—Oil—20" × 24"—Collection Dr. & Mrs. Elton Yasona

Marriage Trio (1952)—Oil—28″ × 14″—Collection Smith-Girard, Stamford, Conn. Reproduced in *Art in America*, 1980

Three Dancers (1966)—Oil—44″ × 36″—Collection Mr. & Mrs. Ronald Paransky

Still Life (1968)—Oil—25″ × 30″—Collection Smith-Girard Stamford, Conn.

Main Street (1945)—Oil—30″ × 45″—Published in *American Artist* magazine, 1980

Portrait of Theresa (1968)—Oil—25″ × 32″—Collection Theresa Bernstein Meyerowitz

Red Horses (1970)—Oil—30″ × 25″—Collection Theresa Bernstein Meyerowitz

Bicycles (1973)—Oil—34″ × 24″—Collection Professor Miriam John & Bill Wilson, Livermore, Calif.

Turkey Pond (1930)—Etching in Color—9″ × 12″—Rosenwald Collection, National Gallery, Washington, D.C.

Sunday Morning (1930s)—Etching in Color—10" × 12"—Rosenwald Collection, National Gallery, Washington, D.C.

List of Reproductions

All Dates and Proportions Are Approximate.

At the Well—Early Drawing (1910)—9" × 12"—Photo by Pamlyn Smith
Drama as a Teacher (1916)—Mural—Oil—45" × 52"—Collection Essau Kaboud—Prix de Rome—Honorable Mention
Self-Portrait (1917)—Oil—22" × 28"
The Immigrant (1918)—Etching—6" × 8"—Photo by Frank Richardson—Collection Mr. & Mrs. John Richardson
Armistice, Day of Peace (1918)—Etching—8" × 10"—Published in *American Artist* magazine, 1980
The Glass of Tea (1919)—Etching—8" × 10"—Photo by Pamlyn Smith
William & Theresa (1921)—Etching—8" × 10"—Photo by Pamlyn Smith—Collection Dr. & Mrs. Edward Ezrick
Long Gloucester, American Venice (1920)—Etching—9" × 12"—Collection Justice Oliver Wendell Holmes
Fishermen at Sunrise (1920)—Etching in Color—9" × 12"—Collection Mr. & Mrs. David Goldman
Little Finnish Girls (1920)—Etching—6" × 8"
Finnish Girls Dancing (1920)—Oil—20" × 24"—Photo by Pamlyn Smith
The Talmudists (1920) Etching—8" × 10"—Photo by Peter Richardson—Collection Mr. & Mrs. John Richardson
The Big Trees (1921)—Etching—9" × 12"—Collection Library of Congress
Boat Ashore (1922)—Etching—8" × 10"
Zionists Meeting in Madison Square Garden (1923)—Etching—8" × 10"—Collection Dr. & Mrs. Bert Berlin
Professor Albert Einstein (1923)—8" × 10"—Etching—Photo by Peter Richardson—Collection Mr. & Mrs. J. Richardson
Justice Oliver Wendell Holmes (1923)—Etching—8" × 10"—Collection Harvard University
Artists of Gloucester (1924)—Oil—42" × 52" Photo by Jean O'Gorman—Private Collection
Early Morning, Gloucester (1924)—Etching—7" × 9"—Collection Professor & Mrs. Samuel Shipman
Dancer Resting (1924)—Etching—8" × 10"—Made for Fox Film Co.—Photo by Pamlyn Smith
Duck Pond (1925)—Etching in Color—8" × 10"—Collection Mr. & Mrs. Jerry Rothstein
Plum Street (1925)—Oil—27" × 35"
Nude with Lily (1928)—15" × 25"—Oil—Photo by Pamlyn Smith—Collection Mrs. Meyerowitz
Fishermen's Dock (1928)—Etching in Color—8" × 10"
New York #1 (1929)—Etching—9" × 12"—Collection New-York Historical Society
Turkey Pond (1930)—Etching in Color—9" × 12"—Rosenwald Collection, National Gallery, Washington, D.C.
Sunday Morning (1930s)—Etching in Color—10" × 12"—Rosenwald Collection, National Gallery, Washington, D.C.
Self-Portrait (1930s)—18" × 22"—Collection Mrs. Meyerowitz—Reproduced in *Current Biography*

Zoe (1930s)—Oil—23″ × 36″—Collection Mrs. Myron Notkin

Fishermen's Wharf (1930)—Oil—50″ × 40″—Photo by Colten—Collection Smith-Girard, Stamford, Conn.

The Harbor (1931)—Etching in Color—8″ × 10″—Photo by Michaels—Collection Mr. & Mrs. Ellie Domeneck

Ready to Sail (1931)—Etching in Color—8″ × 10″—Collection Bethesda Art Gallery

Justice Hugo L. Black (1931)—Etching—8″ × 10″

Justice Owen J. Roberts (1932)—Etching—8″ × 10″

Mother in White Shawl (1932)—Oil—27″ × 35″—Photo by Peter A. Juley—Collection Mr. & Mrs. James Meyerowitz

Paul Revere Still Life (1932)—Oil—20″ × 27″—Collection Mr. & Mrs. Sidney Indeck

Self-Portrait with Four Heads (1933)—Oil—27″ × 35″—Photo by Pamlyn Smith

WPA Mural (1933)—3½′ × 8′—Clinton, Conn., Post Office

Three Fishermen (1935)—Etching in Color—8″ × 10″—Collection Stephen Marks—First Prize, American Color Print Society 1945

The Moors (1935)—Oil—22″ × 28″

The Farm (1935)—9″ × 12″—Etching in Color—Photo by Willett—Collection Pamlyn Smith

New England Street (1935)—Oil—29″ × 37″—Collection Columbus Museum of Art, Georgia

Justice Felix Frankfurter (1935)—Etching—Photo by Pamlyn Smith—Collection Harvard University

East Gloucester (1937)—Oil—30″ × 40″—Collection Mrs. Meyerowitz

Justice Benjamin Cardozo (1937)—Etching in Color—8″ × 10″—Photo by Pamlyn Smith

Justice William O. Douglas (1938)—Etching 8″ × 10″—Collection George Washington University

Justice Harlan Fiske Stone (1938)—Etching—8″ × 10″—Photo by Pamlyn Smith—Collection Harvard University

Self-Portrait (1938)—Oil—20″ × 30″—Collection Mr. & Mrs. Milton Rose

Playmates (1938)—Oil—20″ × 24″—Private Collection

Justice Louis Dembitz Brandeis (1939)—Etching—8″ × 10″—Collection Brandeis University

Horseback Riders (1939)—Oil—23″ × 30″—Collection American British Art Center

Still Life with Iris (1940)—Etching in Color—8″ × 10″—Collection Metropolitan Museum

The Two Resas (1940)—Oil—20″ × 24″—Collection Mona Aarons

The Country Store (1940s)—Oil—20″ × 24″—Photo by Pamlyn Smith—Collection Mrs. Meyerowitz

Inner Harbor (1942)—Oil—19″ × 23″—Collection Mr. & Mrs. John Richardson

Magdalena (1942)—Oil—25″ × 32″—Collection Mr. & Mrs. James Boratgis

Mona (1942)—Oil—25″ × 30″—Private Collection

Exodus (1942)—Oil—40″ × 45″—Collection Jewish Museum, New York City

Fishermen's Wharf (1943)—Oil—34″ × 48″—First Prize North Shore Arts Association, 1943—Collection Mrs. Meyerowitz

The Dictators (1940s)—Oil—20″ × 24″—Photo by Pamlyn Smith—Collection Mrs. Meyerowitz

The Bridle Path (1944)—Etching in Color—8″ × 10″—Collection Mr. & Mrs. Milton Rose

The Masque Ball (1944)—Oil—35″ × 45″—Collection Smith-Girard, Stamford, Conn.

The Encounter (1945)—Lithograph—9″ × 12″

Professor Carl Friedrich (1945)—Oil—25″ × 30″—Collection Mr. Durhan Miller

Main Street (1945)—Oil—30″ × 45″—Published in *American Artist* magazine, 1980

Winnie in the Zoo (1945)—Oil—25″ × 30″—Collection Mr. & Mrs. Arley Pett

New York Mural (1945)—40″ × 50″—Mayor La Guardia's Office, New York City

Jacob K. Javits (1945)—Oil—30" × 36"—Collection Republican Club, New York City
The Smoke Houses (1945)—Watercolor—15" × 19"
The Catch (1947)—Oil—25" × 30"—Collection Dr. & Mrs. Gesedah
Fluctuating Tide (1947)—Oil—25" × 30"—Collection Mrs. Myron Notkin
Road to the Beach (1947)—Oil—20" × 27"—Collection Mrs. Myron Notkin
The Duet (1947)—Oil—28" × 32"—Collection Mr. & Mrs. Paul Geier
The Prophet—Oil—16" × 25"—Collection Dr. Samuel Eidinger
The Finish Line (1948)—Oil—39" × 40"—Collection Mr. & Mrs. Rudy Schaffer
Crow Village (1948)—Oil—25" × 30"—Collection Mrs. Meyerowitz
Self-Portrait (1948)—Oil—30" × 36"
Silver Moon Still Life (1948)—Oil—27" × 35"—Collection Mr. & Mrs. Samuel Godinsky
Gloucester, Norman's Woe (1948)—Oil—30" × 36"—Collection Addison Gilbert Hospital
Abstract Horses (1948)—Oil—27" × 35"—Photo by Peter A. Juley
Floral Still Life (1948)—34" × 26"—Oil—Collection Mr. & Mrs. John Richardson
Adagio (1948)—Oil—13" × 20"—Collection Dr. & Mrs. Samuel Eidinger
The Bread of Toil (1948)—Oil
Henry Hurwitz (1949)—Oil—20" × 24"—Photo by David Lyon Hurwitz—Collection David Lyon Hurwitz
Ipswich Church (1949)—Oil—30" × 36"
In the Garden (1950s)—Oil—19" × 23"—Collection Mr. & Mrs. Arthur Stark
The Cellist (1950)—Oil—17" × 21"—Collection Dr. & Mrs. Samuel Eidinger
Trio (1950)—Oil—9" × 30" × 38"—Collection Mr. & Mrs. Frank Richardson
Theresa Painting (1950)—Oil—25" × 30"—Collection Mrs. Myron Notkin
The Cellist (1950)—Etching in Color—8" × 10"—Photo by John Reynolds—Collection Jesuit Community, Georgetown University
Modern New York (1950)—Etching—9" × 12"—Photo by Pamlyn Smith
The Gallop (1950)—Oil—25" × 35"—Collection Mrs. Stanley Grumbacker
Vladimir Heifetz (1951)—Oil—20" × 36"—Collection Samuel Godinsky
Round Up (1952)—Oil—25" × 35"—Collection Mr. & Mrs. Leonard Marks
Dancing Chassidim (1952)—Drawing—25" × 30"—Collection Ari Barer
The Tomb of David, Jerusalem (1952)—Etching—8" × 10"—Photo by Pamlyn Smith
Music in the Garden (1952)—Oil—30" × 35"—Photo by John F. Mason—Collection Mr. & Mrs. Sol Gold
Rosalyn Tureck (1953)—Oil—20" × 35"—Collection Mrs. Rosalyn Tureck
The Sheltering Tree (1954)—Oil—25" × 30"—Collection Mrs. Myron Notkin
Still Life with Peaches (1955)—Oil—27" × 35"—Collection Dr. & Mrs. Bazalel Levi
The Riders (1955)—20" × 38"—Oil—Photo by Peter A. Juley
Still Life (1955)—Oil—30" × 40"—Collection Smith-Girard—Gold Medal, Rockport Art Association 1970
Invitation to Dance (1956)—Oil—12" × 18"—Collection Mr. & Mrs. Ari Barer
Professor Ithiel da Sola Pool (1956)—Oil—20" × 24"—Photo by Adam da Sola Pool—Collection Professor & Mrs. Ithiel da Sola Pool
The Eyes of Day (1956)—Oil—20" × 24"—Collection Fitchburg Art Museum, Fitchburg, Mass.
Allegro VI (1958)—Oil—20" × 38"—Collection Juley A. Richardson
The Clarinetist (1958)—Oil—18" × 27"—Collection Terra Museum, Evanston, Ill.
The Quartet (1958)—Oil—26" × 29"—Collection Professor Stephen Marks
The Rooster and the Book (1960s)—Oil—30" × 45"—Collection Mr. & Mrs. Harry Sussman
Young Musician (1960s)—Oil—22" × 32"—Photo by Peter A. Juley—Collection Belle Golding
Two Musicians (1960s)—Oil—14" × 25"—Collection Smith-Girard, Stamford, Conn.

Chassidim (1961)—Oil—20″ × 28″—Collection Mr. & Mrs. P. Graicerstein
Frontier Horsemen—Oil—30″ × 46″—Collection Mr. & Mrs. Samuel Raizin
Trio (1963)—Oil—12″ × 16″—Collection Mr. Michael Greenblatt
Chess Players (Marcel Duchamp, William & Theresa) (1964)—Oil—25″ × 30″
Cavalcade (1965)—Oil—27″ × 35″—Photo by Don Soucy—Private Collection
Picadilly Horses (1965)—Oil—20″ × 38″—Collection Dr. & Mrs. Sidney Miller
The Entertainers (1965)—Oil—12″ × 16″
Carnival Dancers (1965)—Oil—54″ × 45″—Photo by Peter A. Juley—Collection Benjamin Stack
Three Dancers (1966)—Oil—40″ × 50″—Collection Mr. & Mrs. Ronald Paransky
Dancing Horses (1968)—Oil—12″ × 16″—Photo by Morris Warman—Collection Mr. & Mrs. Samuel Deutsch
The Hippies (1968)—Oil—25″ × 30″—Photo by Peter A. Juley—Collection Dr. & Mrs. Levine
Still Life (1968)—Oil—27″ × 35″—Collection Smith-Girard, Stamford, Conn.—Lowe Award, Allied Artists 1972
Abstract Horses (1969)—Oil—25″ × 36″—Photo by Peter A. Juley—Collection Dr. & Mrs. Kaufman
Mt. Pleasant Avenue (1975)—24″ × 35″—Photo by Daniel Salo—Collection Elmer Salo
Western Horses (1975)—Oil—25″ × 30″—Collection Smith-Girard, Stamford, Conn.
The Joyful Riders (1975)—Oil—23″ × 28″—Collection Mrs. William Meyerowitz
Still Life with Table (1970s)—Oil—30″ × 40″—Gold Medal, Rockport Art Association 1978
The Cellist (1979)—Oil—20″ × 24″—Collection Dr. Dorothea Sousa

Color Reproductions

Chromatic Scale (1929)—Etching in Color—12″ × 10″—Collection Smith-Girard, Stamford, Conn.
Crucifixion (1929)—Etching in Color—10″ × 12″—Collection Smith-Girard, Stamford, Conn.
Turkey Pond (1930)—Etching in Color—9″ × 12″—Rosenwald Collection, National Gallery, Washington, D.C.
Sunday Morning (1930s)—Etching in Color—10″ × 12″—Rosenwald Collection, National Gallery, Washington, D.C.
Jacob's House, Gloucester (1933)—Watercolor—15″ × 19″—Collection Smith-Girard, Stamford, Conn.
Still Life with Iris (1940)—Etching in Color—8″ × 10″—Collection Metropolitan Museum of Art
Fishermen Mending Nets (1942)—Oil—18″ × 25″—Collection Dr. & Mrs. Elton Yasona
Main Street (1945)—Oil—30″ × 45″—Published in *American Artist* magazine, 1980
Abstract Still Life (1947)—Oil—20″ × 24″—Collection Dr. & Mrs. Elton Yasona
Marriage Trio (1952)—Oil—28″ × 14″—Collection Smith-Girard, Stamford, Conn. Reproduced in *Art in America*, 1980
Three Dancers (1966)—Oil—44″ × 36″—Collection Mr. & Mrs. Ronald Paransky
Portrait of Theresa (1968)—Oil—25″ × 32″—Collection Theresa Bernstein Meyerowitz
Still Life (1968)—Oil—25″ × 30″—Collection Smith-Girard, Stamford, Conn.
Red Horses (1970)—Oil—30″ × 25″—Collection Theresa Bernstein Meyerowitz
Bicycles (1973)—Oil—34″ × 24″—Collection Professor Miriam John & Bill Wilson, Livermore, Calif.

At the Well

Drama as a Teacher

Self-Portrait

The Immigrant

The Glass of Tea

Armistice, Day of Peace

William & Theresa

Long Gloucester, American Venice

Fishermen at Sunrise

Little Finnish Girls

Finnish Girls Dancing

The Talmudists

The Big Trees

Boat Ashore

Zionists Meeting in Madison Square Garden

Professor Albert Einstein

Justice Oliver Wendell Holmes

Artists of Gloucester

Early Morning, Gloucester

Dancer Resting

Duck Pond

Plum Street

Nude with Lily

Fishermen's Dock

New York #1

Turkey Pond

Sunday Morning

Self-Portrait

Zoe

Fishermen's Wharf

The Harbor

Ready to Sail

Justice Hugo L. Black

Justice Owen J. Roberts

Mother in White Shawl

Self-Portrait with Four Heads

Paul Revere Still Life

WPA Mural

Three Fishermen

The Moors

The Farm

New England Street

Justice Felix Frankfurter

East Gloucester

Justice Benjamin Cardozo

Justice William O. Douglas

Justice Harlan Fiske Stone

Self-Portrait

Playmates

Justice Louis Dembitz Brandeis

Horseback Riders

Still Life with Iris

The Two Resas

The Country Store

Inner Harbor

Magdalena

Mona

Exodus

Fishermen's Wharf

The Dictators

The Bridle Path

The Masque Ball

The Encounter

Professor Carl Friedrich

Main Street

Winnie in the Zoo

New York Mural

Jacob K. Javits

The Smoke Houses

The Catch

Fluctuating Tide

Road to the Beach

The Duet

The Prophet

The Finish Line

Crow Village

Self-Portrait

Silver Moon Still Life

Gloucester, Norman's Woe

Abstract Horses

Floral Still Life

Adagio

The Bread of Toil

Henry Hurwitz

Ipswich Church

In the Garden

The Cellist

Trio

Theresa Painting

The Cellist

Modern New York

The Gallop

Vladimir Heifetz

Round Up

Dancing Chassidim

The Tomb of David

Music in the Garden

Rosalyn Tureck

The Sheltering Tree

Still Life with Peaches

Invitation to Dance

The Riders

Still Life

The Eyes of Day

Professor Ithiel de Sola Pool

Allegro VI

The Clarinetist

The Quartet

The Rooster and the Book

Young Musician

Two Musicians

Chassidim

Frontier Horsemen

Trio

Chess Players

Cavalcade

Picadilly Horses

The Entertainers

Carnival Dancers

Three Dancers

Dancing Horses

The Hippies

Still Life

Abstract Horses

Mt. Pleasant Avenue

Western Horses

The Joyful Riders

Still Life with Table

The Cellist

WITHDRAWN